West ~~Sussex Lib~~

WITHD~~RAWN~~

For S~~ale~~

CONTENTS

ALSO BY THE AUTHOR

Haunted Berwick
Haunted Durham
Haunted Newcastle
*The South Shields Poltergeist: One Family's Fight Against an Invisible
Intruder* (with Michael J. Hallowell)

ACKNOWLEDGEMENTS

I would first like to thank my good friend Mike Hallowell, for the help and support he has given me during the compilation of this book, and to Sunderland researcher Alan Tedder, for helping me in ways you couldn't possibly even know. My gratitude goes to Simon Cox and Phil Jeffries for allowing overnight access to their properties. I would also like to thank the Ghosts and Hauntings Overnight Surveillance Team (GHOST) for sharing my adventures with me. Thanks must also go to Drew Bartley and Julie Olley for supplying me with some of the line drawings and illustrations that are printed herein, and to Trevor Yorke for allowing me to reproduce his wonderful sketch of the Battle of Edgehill. Thanks to paranormal writer John Stoker for kindly allowing the reproduction of his text regarding the *Betsy Jane*, and for his information on the rector's ghost of St Peter's Church in Dorchester. Also *Fortean Times* for their information regarding Grainger Street. To everyone I have spoken to, received stories from, and gained information to help me prepare this work, I offer you my sincere thanks. You all know who you are.

My gratitude also goes to my editor Beth Amphlett and the rest of the staff at The History Press.

Finally, I would like to thank you, the reader, for choosing to buy this book. Without good people like yourselves, my work, my writing and my research would all be in vain.

Every effort has been made to trace copyright holders and to obtain their permission for the use of copyright material. I apologise to anyone who has been inadvertently missed out and will gladly receive information enabling me to rectify any error or omission in subsequent editions. Unless otherwise stated, all pictures were taken by Darren W. Ritson.

FAMOUS CHRISTMAS QUOTES

Happy, happy Christmas, that can win us back to the delusions of our childish days; that can recall to the old man the pleasures of his youth; that can transport the sailor and the traveller, thousands of miles away, back to his own fire-side and his quiet home.

Charles Dickens, *The Pickwick Papers*, 1836

A Christmas gambol oft could cheer, the poor man's heart through half the year.

Sir Walter Scott, 'Marmion', 1808

The Church does not superstitiously observe days, merely as days, but as memorials of important facts. Christmas might be kept as well upon one day of the year as another; but there should be a stated day for commemorating the birth of our Saviour, because there is danger that what may be done on any day, will be neglected.

Dr Samuel Johnson

I will honour Christmas in my heart, and try to keep it all the year.

Charles Dickens, *A Christmas Carol*, 1843

Charles Dickens, the author of
A Christmas Carol, *in 1852.*
(Courtesy of Wikipedia)

At Christmas I no more desire a rose than wish a snow in May's new-fangled shows; but like of each thing that in season grows.

William Shakespeare, *Love's Labour's Lost*, 1598

I have always thought of Christmas time, when it has come round, as a good time; a kind, forgiving, charitable time; the only time I know of, in the long calendar of the year, when men and women seem by one consent to open their shut-up hearts freely, and to think of people below them as if they really were fellow passengers to the grave, and not another race of creatures bound on other journeys.

Charles Dickens, *A Christmas Carol*, 1843

INTRODUCTION

Do you believe in ghosts? This is a question that is becoming far more frequently asked these days, due to the rise in interest in supernatural activity and matters that are deemed 'paranormal'. There is no doubt in my mind that apparitions are seen – indeed I have seen them myself – but are they really the dead returning or is there another explanation for them?

Over the past ten years I have travelled around the UK investigating hundreds of haunted locations and chatting with people who own haunted places, and other people that have seen, or experienced, ghosts for themselves. The stories they tell are often quite amazing. On top of that, I have dedicated hundreds upon hundreds of hours (I kid you not) sitting in dark and spooky haunted locations waiting for the spectral visitors to make their presences known, sometimes with startling results. It has been a real pleasure and the work is only just beginning.

Christmas has long been associated with ghosts and I have always wanted to put together my own compilation of chilling Christmas accounts. There are many others that have walked this wonderful road before me, including M.R. James, Sir Arthur Conan Doyle, the great Charles Dickens and my good friend Mike Hallowell. So when I was approached by The History Press and asked if I would be prepared to pen a volume on festive phantoms I jumped at the chance – I mean, what self-respecting ghost hunter and author wouldn't?

I remember when I was very young, on Christmas Eve, after my brother and I had eventually dropped off to sleep, my mother and father would cover the settee and chairs with wonderful gifts. Of course, when we awoke the following morning and dashed down the stairs we would burst open the living room door to find that 'he' had been; it was magical. I never questioned where these gifts came from as I knew it was Father Christmas who had brought them. He must have, because searching the house high and low prior to 24 December in search of hidden gifts always yielded nothing, no matter where I looked. Being a child and being wrapped up in the whole magical experience, I didn't really question those inconsistencies that are so obvious to me now. Children simply revel in the whole Christmas experience.

The traditional home Christmas tree, festooned with tinsel, lights and small gifts.

It must be said, however, that Christmas is also quite a sad time for me, for it was on 25 December 1993 when I lost my grandmother, May Bower, after she had fought a long battle against lung cancer. Losing a friend or a family member is bad enough to begin with, no matter how much time you are given to prepare for it, but to lose a loved one on Christmas Day – a time for rejoicing and being with your family – is probably one of the worst things that could happen.

On 25 March 1994, three months after her sad death, a very strange thing happened to me. While sitting at home in my living room, eating my breakfast of boiled eggs and toast, the three photographs of my gran, which we had placed up on shelves and on our mantelpiece, fell over all at the same time! I heard three thumps in quick succession and when I looked up to see what it was I noticed it was the photographs. How the three pictures – which were in frames and on stands – could fall over right at the same time eludes me, leaving me with the conclusion that it was just gran popping in to say hello, and letting me know that

Mr Fezziwig's Ball; an illustration by John Leech depicting the ghost of Christmas past. (Courtesy of Wikipedia)

Thomas Nast's depiction of a 'Merry old Santa' from 1881. (Courtesy of Wikipedia)

everything was well. The pictures had fallen over at 7.30 a.m., the exact time we discovered gran had slipped away from us three months earlier.

So I began my research and started to collect spine-chilling accounts of ghosts that occur around the festive season. There are plenty to discuss I might add; the ghostly butterfly of the Theatre Royal in Bath, the troubled souls of the starving children at Bramber Castle in Sussex, the phantom armies at Edgehill, North Road station in Darlington, north-east England, the apparition of Kathleen Breaks in Blackpool and many, many more can be found within the pages of this new and exciting volume.

Over the years I have personally carried out many ghost vigils in reputedly haunted locations, with a small percentage of these overnight investigations being at Christmas time. I don't know what it is about investigating haunted properties in and around Yuletide (or Ghoultide, as some folk prefer to call it), but it does have a certain eerie quality to it that most other investigations often lack. Perhaps it is the atmosphere that the long and cold winter nights bring? Could it be Jack Frost as he makes his presence felt across the land by leaving in his wake a white layer of sparkling aesthetic beauty which, when seen in full moonlight, looks most enchanting, yet remarkably spooky. Perhaps it's because Christmas time follows shortly after Halloween? A friend of mine, Drew Bartley, often says that 'from September through to January is ghost hunting season' and I know exactly what he means. Of course Drew and I realise that ghosts are felt and seen all of the time, regardless of what month it may be, but we both agree that there is just something 'mysteriously paranormal' about the last quarter of the year and so I have included a small slice of my Christmas investigations in this volume to give the reader a chance to learn of some brand new, never-before-read-about ghosts that inhabit all sorts of weird and wonderful places around the season of good will.

Jack Frost, as he works his magic across the land. (Courtesy of Wikipedia)

Ghosts are most certainly an integral part of the festive season and have been even more so since the release of Charles Dickens' famous novel, *A Christmas Carol*, back in December 1843. In fact, I recently read in a magazine that Christmas Eve can boast more apparitions than any other night of the year – even Halloween! Ghosts, to me, are a wonderful part of our Christmas traditions, as essential as Santa Claus, Christmas presents, seasonal greetings cards, turkey and pulling crackers. The renowned author and ghost hunter Elliott O'Donnell (1872–1965) was also a great believer in Christmas ghosts and spent a lot of his time during the festive season searching for them. By all accounts, he was rarely disappointed.

Now, my dear reader, all that remains for you to do is to sink comfortably in your most inviting armchair and pour yourself a drink. Prepare yourself by turning down the lights and locking the doors – to make sure you won't be disturbed – and begin to leaf through the pages that follow. Be warned, don't think for a moment that these tales are embellished or even untrue ... on the contrary, they are all, to the best of my knowledge, authentic accounts. Ghosts, my dear friends, are real ... so, if you happen to hear an unexplained bump, or feel an unusual chilling draught, then maybe, just maybe, you are not alone.

Merry Christmas, my dear reader.

Darren W. Ritson, 2010

one
FICTIONAL
CHRISTMAS GHOSTS

There's something about Christmas that lends itself to stories of spectres dragging balls and chains or wispy, ethereal females – often headless – sporting diaphanous white gowns as they float through the hallway of some stately mansion or other. Christmas is paradise for the tellers of ghostly tales.

Perhaps the classic example is Charles Dickens' *A Christmas Carol*, in which Scrooge is transported hither and thither by a spirit from the world beyond and forced to confront rather negative aspects of his behaviour – and their potential consequences. As just about everyone knows, *A Christmas Carol* is a wonderful morality tale. However, what many people don't realise about Dickens is that he penned a whole raft of similar stories, including *The Chimes*, *The Cricket on the Hearth*, *The Battle of Life* and *The Haunted Man*. A beautifully bound edition of these – *The Christmas Books* – was published in 1852.

Later writers would capitalise on Dickens' characters. Playwright Jeff Goode went on to pen *Marley's Ghost*, a stage play which was essentially a prequel to *A Christmas Carol*. Goode's play centres around a seven-year spiritual sojourn undertaken by Jacob Marley, beginning with his burial and culminating with his appearance to Ebenezer Scrooge.

An 1843 illustration by John Leech of Jacob Marley visiting Ebenezer Scrooge on Christmas Eve. (Courtesy of Wikipedia)

The advent of the television age was a boon for Christmas ghost stories. Back in the 1970s, the BBC produced eight programmes in a series entitled *A Ghost Story for Christmas*. The tales, predominantly the brainchild of M.R. James, included, *Lost Hearts*, *The Treasure of Abbot Thomas*, *The Signalman* and *The Ice House*, but they were not for the faint of heart. A radio version of the series was broadcast shortly afterwards.

Christmas ghost stories had long since made the transition to the cinema screen, of course. Back in 1957, Random House released the Dr Seuss book, *How the Grinch Stole Christmas!*; a morality tale, this time for children, which warns against the exploitation and commercialisation of the festive season. With not a little irony, the book was turned into a hugely successful cartoon animation in 1966. In 2000 a feature film of the same title was released (but without the exclamation mark) and back in 1994 a musical version made its début in a Minneapolis theatre. *How the Grinch Stole Christmas* wasn't exactly a ghost story, of course, but it certainly helped cement the relationship between Christmas and the supernatural.

In 1988, the actor Bill Murray starred in the film *Scrooged*, which offered a new take on the idea behind Dickens' novel. Old themes repackaged can offer a new and refreshing twist on things, and the movie reinforced the 'ghosts at Christmas' theme to a whole new generation.

Returning to the musical theme, the band Trans-Siberian Orchestra have packaged together numerous Christmas songs, including those used in the made-for-television movie *The Ghosts of Christmas Eve*, with Michael Crawford. The fusion of both was nothing less than superb.

To understand why the relationship between ghosts and the Christmas season is such a natural one, we need to look back at the origins of Christmas itself. Based on an ancient Roman festival, Christmas successfully fused the Pagan concept of merrymaking with the birth of Christ. One cannot really partake of Christmas without enjoying oneself, and neither can one truly revel in Christmas festivities without at least acknowledging that there is a deeply spiritual platform underpinning everything. The Christmas ghost story provides both aspects perfectly. *A Christmas Carol*, for instance, is one of the most entertaining books ever written, and yet it also sucks the reader into acknowledging a life beyond the world we currently inhabit, the religious virtue of doing good to others and the penitence of the sinner. Other novels, films and plays have echoed the same theme.

The 1990 movie *Home Alone*, starring Macaulay Culkin, tells the story of a young boy accidentally left behind when his family flies to Europe for their Christmas holiday. Culkin embodies the modern equivalent of the unhappy child and, as in Dickens' tale, it all comes good in the end.

Arguably, because Christmas draws us, consciously or unwittingly, closer to the spiritual world than we might get at other times of the year, ghosts, spectres and phantasms inevitably intrude into the picture. There is something perfectly *natural* about seeing a ghost at Christmas time, or at least reading about one.

Sometimes it's hard to draw a distinction between true Christmas ghost tales and fictional ones. My colleague Mike Hallowell once penned a seemingly fictional story about a ghostly sailor who appeared to a motorist one Christmas outside a pub, and the driver, not realising the chap was 'not of this world', so to speak, gave the phantom a lift. Eerily, it turned out later that a real ghost – that of a phantom sailor – had been seen outside the very same pub that Mike had included in his fictional story. Was this a case of 'life imitating art', or the other way around?

It seems that there are a number of unwritten rules about Christmas ghost stories that most writers, consciously or otherwise, adhere to. Good Christmas ghost tales normally contain a moral; a psychological prompt which leaves the reader pondering over their own life or behaviour. Another unwritten

Scrooge being visited by the ghost of Christmas present; an illustration by John Leech from 1843. (Courtesy of Wikipedia)

rule is that they should either have a happy ending or an absolutely awful one. Like Tiny Tim, who started out with the prospect of having no Christmas lunch and ended up with a feast, there are no half measures. Christmas ghost stories are meant to uplift the reader or, alternatively, terrify them.

The setting is important too. A good Christmas ghost story is unlikely to be set on the moon, in Jamaica or in the Australian outback; these environments lack snow, cobbled streets and dimly-lit gas lamps. Charles Dickens would never have dreamed of sending Marley's Ghost to see Scrooge in Buenos Aires or Seville, although he might just have got away with a barren, windswept setting on the Isle of Skye. There, whistling winds and bleak moors would have made a passable substitute for the authentic setting.

The length of the story is also significant. The vast majority of Christmas ghost stories are short ones and not full-length novels. There is a good reason for this: Christmas ghost stories are supposed to leave the reader wanting more. Too much detail deadens the imagination and makes a ghost tale seem mundane. You can get away with writing an ordinary ghost tale of great length, but not a Christmas one.

Sometimes it is possible to blend a number of different themes and media together with truly fascinating results. American band The Killers made a now-legendary track called 'Don't Shoot Me Santa', which is musically sublime, hilariously funny and mildly unsettling in the way it distorts the image of Santa Claus from kindly gift-giver into psychotic killer. The song would stand on its own, but coupled with the accompanying video it takes the listener/viewer into a surreal world every bit as disorientating as the one Scrooge found himself in. And yet, in some ways, it is the same world: the Dark Side of Christmas. There are no ghosts in 'Don't Shoot Me Santa', but there are certainly watchful, brooding spirits. True to form, both the soundtrack and the video have a happy ending.

Although it's possible to look at the imagery of the typical Christmas ghost story and find all sorts of pop psychology in

The ghost of Christmas future; an illustration by John Leech from 1843.
(Courtesy of Wikipedia)

there, we shouldn't dig too deeply. Christmas ghost stories in the world of entertainment are, primarily, meant to be enjoyed. Even Dickens would have settled for someone merely enjoying *A Christmas Carol* or *The Haunted Man* even if reading them didn't prove to be a life-changing experience.

Since the 1940s, film makers have had at their disposal an ever-growing battery of Christmas songs to use as a musical backdrop to horror and haunting movies. The truly weird thing is that it doesn't seem to matter which ones you use; a Christmas song is a Christmas song, and would be strangely appropriate whether used in the comedy *National Lampoon's Christmas Vacation* or in the supernatural slice'n'dice horror *Carnage Over Christmas*, in which a spectre goes on the rampage in a college campus with a cleaver.

Why do Christmas ghost stories in the field of entertainment have such a profound effect upon us? It isn't hard to figure out. Although ghost stories and Yuletide enjoy a very happy marriage, Christmas is supposed to be the time when, if only for a few days, we enjoy 'peace on earth and good will to all men'. *Nothing* is supposed to go wrong at Christmas or disturb our sensibilities. A Christmas ghost disturbs us all the more, then, for it is set in a misleading context. Film makers are well aware of the shock value of putting something evil in a benign setting, for it emphasises the bad all the more. Movies such as *Black Christmas* (1974), *Silent Night, Evil Night* (1974), *Christmas Evil* (1980) and *Don't Open Till Christmas* (1984), all assault the senses with unspeakable horrors, they're just horrors draped with tinsel and lights, that's all.

But not all Christmas ghost stories are so graphic and obvious. Sometimes, it is what you don't see that frightens you. Just when you're getting to the last paragraph of the tale and sanity seems to be returning to the world within the pages of the book, something terrible happens. In the last sentence – or perhaps dying seconds of the film – the door creaks open, the footsteps in the attic start again or the face returns to peer in at the window. And then you know it isn't *really* over. You may be terrified, but at least you can console yourself with the knowledge that the author/playwright/ director has left the way open for a sequel. If your nerves can stand it, of course.

Christmas is a crowd-puller in the entertainment world, and so are ghost stories. Together they make a potent mix. Of course, there is also plenty of evidence to suggest that the connection between ghosts and Christmas is not just confined to the world of fiction …

two
GHOSTS
AT CHRISTMAS

CHRISTMAS EVE KITTY, BLACKPOOL

On Christmas Eve 1919, the lifeless body of Kathleen Breaks – or Kitty as she was known locally – was found amongst the sand dunes near Lytham Road not far from Blackpool. Early indications showed that Kitty had been shot; not once, but three times at point-blank range with a revolver. Kitty had been seeing a local man, Frederick Rothwell Holt, and, by all accounts, their relationship was a rough and ready one. The element of danger, along with the thought of making out with a 'bad boy' appeals to some women. But a lot of these relationships end in tragedy – just like this one.

A fight or an argument must have ensued during their last night together. What it was about we can only speculate. Perhaps Kitty pleaded with Fredrick to sort himself out and 'go straight' so they could set up together properly and honestly? Perhaps Kitty had told her lover she was pregnant, which could have brought on fear and resentment on his part towards Kitty, with the only way out for him being to get rid of her … and the baby. No one knows for certain, but, whatever did occur that fateful night, it resulted in the brutal murder of the young woman.

Holt's revolver was found near the body.

It is said that Holt's bloodstained gloves, along with his service revolver – the one used to fire the fatal shots – and a footprint that matched his footwear, was discovered not far from where Kitty was found. This incriminating evidence led to the subsequent arrest of Holt and his execution shortly afterwards. Over the years many holiday makers and Blackpool locals have claimed to have seen the miserable itinerant spectre of this young woman, usually on Christmas Eve (the anniversary of the discovery of her body), as she meanders slowly along the sand dunes in a dazed and bewildered fashion. Her bullet wounds drip with fresh blood that stains her dirty clothes, sending chills down the spines of those who encounter her.

THE GHOST OF
NORTH ROAD STATION, DARLINGTON

North Road railway station in Darlington was the scene of a spectacular ghost apparition that occurred one freezing cold December night. The railway station, which is now a popular museum, once served the Darlington to Stockton rail service and has had a reputation for being haunted ever since that fateful night.

A suicide is believed to have taken place there sometime between the late 1840s and 1890. It is thought that one Thomas Winter took his own life by shooting himself in the head in the gents' lavatory, and it is his spectre that is now said to haunt the station. Winter's body was found in the station by railway staff, whereupon he was taken to the on-site cellars where he was laid until they were able to move him to the local mortuary or some other place of rest.

Blackpool Tower. It was in Blackpool where, in 1919, Kathleen Breaks (Kitty) was found murdered in the sand dunes. (Courtesy of Jackie Hallowell)

An artist's impression of Kitty Breaks as she wanders through the sand dunes, shot and bleeding. (Julie Olley)

North Road railway station in Darlington, the scene of an amazing ghost story from the 1800s. (Darren W. Ritson and Mike Hallowell)

North Road station platform. (Darren W. Ritson and Mike Hallowell)

The body was taken to the cellars until it could be moved to the local mortuary.

One cold winter's night in December 1890 a man was observed coming in and out of the cellar area by a night-watchman who was on duty at the time. The night-watchman described the intruder as 'wearing old-fashioned attire, including an old style hat and coat'. 'With him,' he stated, 'was a large black dog.' The night-watchman decided to approach the intruder and challenge him, but something was to occur that would change the life of the watchman and give the station its ghostly reputation.

What happened next no one knows for sure but it was reported that the mysterious figure, for some reason, took a swing at the night-watchman and knocked him to the ground. The watchman got back to his feet and quickly took a swing back at the intruder. To his utter shock, he found that his fist and arm went straight through the mystery man. The punch connected not with the stranger's face, but the wall behind it, resulting in bruised and scrapped knuckles; he was not having a good night!

To make things worse, the spectre, or whatever it was, set his fierce canine companion upon the night-watchman and stood gazing by as it bit and mauled him savagely. After what seemed like a lifetime for the watchman, the mystery figure called the animal off, whereupon they both walked away and straight through the cellar wall. The night-watchman picked himself up, brushed himself down and headed back to the

The man's dog bit and mauled the night-watchman savagely.

The author by the glass that now covers the old entrance hatch to the cellar where the ghost of North Road station was seen all those years ago. (Darren W. Ritson and Mike Hallowell)

The porters' entrance to the cellar at North Road station. (Darren W. Ritson and Mike Hallowell) office to recuperate from his terrifying ordeal. Upon telling his story he was ridiculed and scorned, with people suggesting that he was merely drunk on the job. It was only when they discovered that the night-watchman was a devout teetotaller and a god-fearing man that his story was taken seriously.

The Incorporated Society for Psychical Research (SPR) were convinced that the story held some validity and sent an investigator up from London to document the case. After interviewing the witness and conducting his research, he left the North East of England convinced that what went on that cold, dark December night was a *bona fide* paranormal incident. To the best of my knowledge, this spectral apparition has never been seen again, although ghost hunters in the North East insist paranormal activity still occurs at the station from time to time.

And maybe it does; after a visit to the station in late February 2010 with Mike Hallowell, and after a lengthily chat with the museum manager, Dave Tetlow, we discovered that the museum is not just host to one ghost, but three. A man in red is said to have been seen by many children in the engine compartment of the Tennant 1463 locomotive. He is said to look at the controls of the engine before disappearing into thin air. The third ghost is a female and is known as the Third-class Carriage Ghost. She is seen sitting in the back of a third-class carriage that was built in 1865. This Victorian spectre is thought to be responsible for many strange noises that seems to emanate from this area of the museum.

The museum is fascinating to say the least and my trip there was very enjoyable. However, the cellar ghost has certainly left its mark on the building, leaving me in no doubt that this particular Christmas ghost is one of the most frightening I have ever come across.

THE PHANTOM BUTTERFLY OF BATH

The Theatre Royal in Bath is said to be the most haunted theatre in Britain. This beautiful Georgian theatre was built over 200 years ago and is home to a phantom butterfly that flutters around the theatre during performances at Christmas.

The first sighting was around 1948, when a new production was being performed. The dancers in the show were all dressed as butterflies and were doing a ballet number when all of a sudden a butterfly appeared from nowhere and fluttered about the stage, much to the joy and surprise of the audience. Over the years the phantom butterfly has appeared on countless occasions during productions and shows, fluttering around the theatre and then simply disappearing. The butterfly has become something of a good luck charm and is said to appear before certain productions, indicating the show will be a great success.

An illustration of the phantom butterfly said to haunt the Theatre Royal in Bath during Christmas performances. (Mike Hallowell, Thunderbird Craft and Media)

The theatre is also home to two other ghosts. A lady in a grey dress is said to walk the halls and passageways of the theatre after she killed herself in the 1880s, after discovering that her husband had killed her lover, and the ghost of a doorman in eighteenth-century garb is often seen. No one knows who he is.

THE GHOST CHILDREN OF
BRAMBER CASTLE, SUSSEX

Not much is left of Bramber Castle. In fact, apart from infinitesimal traces of the curtain wall in the north-east area of the location, the wall of the gatehouse tower is the only segment of the castle that survives. Rising almost 75ft in height, it stands alone in a secluded beauty spot, surrounded by forest and grassland, not far from the village of Bramber. The word Bramber derives from the Saxon word *Brymmburh*, meaning fortified hill.

The castle was built to safeguard the large port that was situated on the River Adur and continued to do so until the castle was attacked and subsequently destroyed by the Parliamentary forces. William De Breone or Braose owned it during the reign of King John and, after William fell from the king's favour, John ordered that William's children should be taken from him and held captive

An illustration by Wenzel Hollar showing Bramber and its castle between 1607 and 1677. (Courtesy of Wikipedia)

An artist's impression of Bramber Castle and the ghosts of the children that have been seen there looking for food on Christmas Day. (Julie Olley)

at Windsor Castle. When William heard that King John's men were on their way he quickly fled to Ireland with his family, in the hope of a peaceful life, but it was not to be. They were soon captured and returned to Windsor Castle and, as punishment to William (and an effort to deter anyone else from betraying the monarch), the king imprisoned William's four children and starved them to death.

Of course, local legend claims that the area surrounding the castle and the village is haunted, and it is believed that it is the wretched ghosts of William's children that haunt the area. They are said to be sad and gaunt-looking as they scramble around the place in search of bread. On Christmas Day they have also been spotted begging for food, although why they appear to beg on 25 December nobody knows.

THE CARLISLE DEVIL DOG

Devil Dogs or Phantom Hounds are said to roam the country from John O'Groats to Land's End. Wherever you are in the UK (or abroad for that matter), you can be rest assured that there is a traditional local name for the hell hound that frequents the area. In Scotland ghost dogs are known as the Muckle Black Tyke. In Wales they are Gwyllgi (meaning dog of darkness). In the Midlands the black dog ghost is known as the Hooter, and in Yorkshire it is a Barguest. In Staffordshire it is known locally as Padfoot, while in East Anglia (more specifically Norfolk) it is Black Shuck, or Old Shuck.

In the nineteenth century, a blacksmith by
the name of John Carter made the decision
to depart from his London home and move
to Carlisle, where he had the chance of
much better-paid employment with a job
that also had good prospects. The chance
to better his own life and that of his wife
seemed too good to miss, but it was a
decision he would later come to regret.
The Carter family arrived in Carlisle on
Christmas Eve and rented a coach to
take them to the nearby village, where
they would live. They were hoping to
be settled into their new home in time
for Yuletide. As the coach, driven by a
rather well-dressed gentleman, took off
through the countryside, John Carter noticed how incredibly
foggy it was becoming.

The fog came in thick and fast, but this didn't seem to bother the
driver, who appeared to have a preference for riding at breakneck
speed. At one point the carriage almost careered off the road as it
manoeuvred round a sharp corner, but still the coachman used his
whip to drive the horse on ever faster. Carter, very much alarmed
at this point, shouted for the driver to slow down.

'Nay, sire! I daren't! Should I slow the coach now a bad thing
will befall us, and no mistake!'

Carter, however, kept shouting at the driver, insisting that he
go slower and, eventually, the man agreed, but told the blacksmith
that the result would be upon his own head.

Not long after the coach had slowed down, Carter was
horror-struck to see a terrible dog-like creature racing alongside
the carriage. It was a large, black dog with 'evil, glowing eyes
and a lolling tongue'. Every now and then the hound would
rear up on its hind legs and paw at the carriage, as if trying to
get inside.

The coach was driven by a well-dressed gentleman.

'Go faster! Go faster!' cried the terrified blacksmith, as his wife shrieked with fear.

'Do you see now, sire? Do you see why I did not want to slow down the carriage?'

John Carter could see all too clearly and now fully understood. Now, instead of going slower, he begged the coachman to speed up as much as he could.

Mile after mile the carriage thundered through the Cumbrian countryside and the thick, nauseating fog. On occasions, the spectral dog – for that's what it was – would fall behind, but only moments later it would, to their horror, catch up again. Eventually the coach approached a river and the driver attempted to guide it over a narrow bridge. Alas, the coach was too wide and became stuck on the bridge, causing the driver to shout, 'Now we're done!' Without hesitation, the howling, slobbering dog began to paw at the carriage door with such strength that it was only a matter of time before it shattered. In desperation, the coach driver cracked his whip at the beast, causing it to fall from the bridge into the frozen river.

The coachman, blacksmith and his wife watched in relief, as the demonic spectre was washed away in the ice-cold current. Eventually the coach was freed from the narrow bridge and continued on its journey. Neither Carter nor his wife ever went near that bridge again, in case they should encounter the 'hound

The Carlisle Devil Dog. (Drew Bartley)

from hell' once more. The driver told the blacksmith and his wife that the phantom dog had roamed the area for generations, and that locals were so frightened of it they were forbidden to mention the beast in public. That was why he set off on the journey with such tremendous speed.

Tales of eerie dogs with glowing eyes are very common indeed, and there are more *bona fide* accounts of phantom black dogs than you may think. Of course, it's easy to take them all with a pinch of salt, but, who knows, Hooter, Black Shuck, Padfoot, Barguest, whatever he is called, he may be waiting for you, my friend, the next time you decide to venture out on a dark winter's night.

THE GHOST OF GRAINGER STREET, NEWCASTLE-UPON-TYNE

William T. Stead's *Real Ghost Stories* (1891) tells the fascinating story of a north-eastern man who was so desperate to see his pictures, which were taken at a photography shop on Grainger Street in Newcastle-upon-Tyne, that he actually went and attempted to pick them up. That doesn't sound so strange does it? But, he seemingly went to the store and asked for his pictures while he was lying on his death bed 7 miles away! Let me explain …

The story begins on one bitterly cold afternoon in December 1890. Some versions suggest it was on 6 December, while others that it was 16 December. Whatever the actual date, we can be sure that the event occurred during the run up to the Christmas of 1890.

A certain Mr J. T. Thompson arrived at the shop on Grainger Street to have his picture taken by the local and renowned

The shop on Grainger Street in Newcastle-upon-Tyne that was home to James Dickinson's photography shop in 1890. (Courtesy of Mike Hallowell, Thunderbird Craft and Media)

A selection of six photographs was taken.

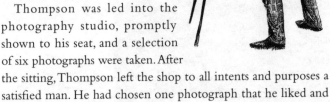

photographer James Dickinson. Dickinson suggested that, as he was not busy at that moment, Thompson could sit for his photograph there and then, as opposed to arranging another time slot for the sitting.

Thompson was led into the photography studio, promptly shown to his seat, and a selection of six photographs were taken. After the sitting, Thompson left the shop to all intents and purposes a satisfied man. He had chosen one photograph that he liked and had subsequently placed his order.

A few weeks later, on 3 January 1891, James Dickinson arrived at his shop to open for business. It was his first day back after the Christmas and New Year break and he was eager to get started. An employee of Dickinson had telephoned him earlier to explain that he was ill and unable to attend work, resulting in Dickinson arriving at his store one hour earlier than he would have usually done. Had he turned up at his normal time of 9 a.m. instead of 8 a.m., he would have missed his chance of being a key witness in one of Victorian England's most bewildering ghost encounters.

As Dickinson was preparing for the day to come, a young man entered the shop. 'Good morning,' he said. 'I have come to see if my photograph is ready.'

'Good morning, sir,' replied Dickinson, 'and your name is?'

'Thompson, J. T. Thompson.'

'And what is your address?' asked Dickinson.

'William Street, Hebburn, Tyne and Wear.'

Dickinson asked the man if he could see his receipt, to which Thompson replied he did not have it with him. However, Thompson had enough identification papers with him to satisfactorily prove to the photographer that he was who he said

J. T. Thompson, taken from W. T. Stead's Real Ghost Stories. (Grant Richards, 1897)

he was. Dickinson then asked Thompson if he could come back in a few hours, when his assistant would be in, as he was extremely busy. Thompson replied in the most strange way, saying, 'Look, I have been travelling all night to get here and I cannot come back.'

Thompson looked wretchedly ill and very tired to say the least; because of this, Dickinson decided to offer him a compromise. But, before Dickinson had a chance to say anything, Thompson had turned around and stormed off.

'Can I post the picture to you?' Dickinson asked the man as he left the shop, but he received no answer. Thompson left the shop, slamming the door behind him, and disappeared into Grainger Street. Dickinson decided that he had better do something to appease the man in order to keep his custom. A good customer is a happy customer, so they say, so Dickinson decided that he should post out Thompson's photograph to his house, without charge for the postage or his picture.

When his other assistant, Miss Simon, arrived for work, Dickinson told her what had occurred and asked her to dig out

Thompson's ordered photograph and pop it in the post. Miss Simon was puzzled. She explained to Dickinson that an elderly man had visited the shop yesterday (which was the Friday) and had asked about the same photograph. She went on to tell this gentleman that, due to the adverse weather conditions, they were three weeks behind with their work and his pictures would not be ready for another week or so.

Dickinson was now puzzled. If someone had been in on Friday querying the picture, then why would someone else, presumably another family member, be calling in the following day? One would have presumed the elder of the two, who came in first, would have told the other one that the picture was not ready.

Regardless, Dickinson now thought to himself that it was about time this man had his photograph so he set about this task as his main priority. He asked his assistant who was printing Thompson's order, to which she replied no one was. She pointed to a pile of negatives that had been sitting on the table for almost two weeks and said that Thompson's picture was in amongst them.

Upon checking the negative, Dickinson was sure that the man in the picture was the same chap who had been in the shop that morning. Although the man had been wearing a top hat and coat when he had called, neither of which he'd worn when the photograph was taken, Dickinson had no difficulty in recognising that it was the same person.

Two days later, Dickinson was in his studio working hard and had still not found the time to complete Thompson's picture. He decided to get this order out of the way first, and made his way down to the shop to retrieve the negative. Much to his dismay, he could not find it and asked Miss Simon to retrieve it from wherever she had placed it last. Miss Simon eventually found a batch of negatives which contained Thompson's picture, but, upon collecting them and passing them all to Dickinson, she managed to somehow drop the plates all over the floor.

Every negative plate survived the mishap bar one – yes, you've guessed it, Thompson's plate. Out of a huge collection of glass

plates Thompson's picture was the only one to be destroyed.
The glass negative had broken in two, straight across the sitter's
head. Dickinson asked Miss Simon to write to Mr Thompson
and request that he come in for another sitting. 'And make sure
to tell him that we'll recompense him for his time and trouble,'
he added. (Bear in mind that another five pictures of Thompson
were in existence at this time, but it was the one good picture that
Thompson had wanted that was smashed. A second sitting was
now the only option.)

A few days later, Dickinson was again working in his studio,
when he heard his assistant call for him. She announced that
a gentleman had arrived to see him about the broken plate.
Thinking it was J.T. Thompson, he asked his assistant to send him
up to the studio at once for his resit. His assistant's voice was heard
yelling up the stairs once more, 'You don't understand, sir. Mr
Thompson is dead.'

Dickinson hurried down the stairs into the main shop to
be greeted by the elderly chap who had called at the shop the
previous Friday. It was Thompson's father. He confirmed that
his son, J.T. Thompson, had recently died at home of an illness.
Dickinson commented upon the fact that the illness must have
come on very quick and severe, as he only saw him in the shop
last week. Thompson's father replied by saying that he couldn't
possibly have seen him last week because at the time his son was
at home, bedridden and at death's door. In fact, he died on the
Saturday afternoon.

Dickinson was certain it was Thompson whom he had seen,
and, furthermore, he had the note in his order book to prove it. As
the elderly Mr Thompson was in distress, Dickinson asked him to
call back a week later, whereupon they could clear this matter up.
Mr Thompson agreed. A week passed and Mr Thompson returned
to the store and spoke with Dickinson again. What he said was
most astounding. In the week leading up to J.T. Thompson's
death he had been taken seriously ill. Soon he became delirious
and was unable to speak any sense whatsoever. He had ranted

*James Dickinson of
Grainger Street, taken
from W.T. Stead's* Real
Ghost Stories. *(Grant
Richards, 1897)*

incoherently about his 'photograph' and insisted he would not be
happy until he had it. On Friday afternoon his father had gone to
Newcastle to retrieve the picture, and this was when Miss Simon
had first encountered the elderly man.

Upset at not being able to get his son's picture for him, he
returned home and informed him. The following day, at 2 p.m.,
J.T. Thompson died. He had not left the house, simply because
he was unable to do so, and his family also stayed by his bedside
in the days leading up to his death. However, the note in the
order book, combined with the testimony of the witnesses –
James Dickinson and a young assistant who had been removing
the grille from the door when Thompson had entered – left no
doubt that J.T. Thompson had been in the store that Saturday
morning in an attempt to pick up his photograph. And yet there
was a multitude of witnesses who testified that, at the time the
man had supposedly visited Dickinson's shop in Grainger Street,
he was actually on his deathbed and passed away just a few hours
later.

William T. Stead, a North Tyneside man who was deeply interested in spiritualism and the paranormal, thoroughly investigated the incident and refers to this anomalous sighting as a 'thought-body'. Nowadays a 'thought-body' is better known to researchers as a 'crisis apparition'. A crisis apparition is, theoretically, the 'ghost' of a living person who desperately needs to take care of some unfinished business before they move on. If they are physically incapable of doing it themselves, then they may project a 'psychic' double to perform their errand for them. This most certainly seems to be the case here.

I will leave the last words to Mr W.T. Stead:

> We may turn it which way we please, there is no hypothesis which will fit the facts except the assumption that there is such a thing as a Thought Body, capable of locomotion and speech, which can transfer itself wherever it pleases, clothing itself with whatever clothes it desires to wear, which are phantasmal like itself. Short of that hypothesis, I do not see any explanation possible; and yet, if we admit that hypothesis, what an immense vista of possibilities is opened up to our view!

THE TOBY CARVERY COACH AND FOUR, SOUTH TYNESIDE

The Toby Carvery is a public house with a long and fascinating history. Formerly known as the Britannia Inn, this South Tyneside pub is thought to be one of the oldest drinking establishments in this particular region. Standing proud at the junction of Boldon Lane and Sunderland Road, this ancient old-world pub is a large and steadfast building, reminiscent of the old fortresses and castles.

The Toby Carvery was originally built as a coaching inn some time in the seventeenth century. An original stone fireplace in the

The Toby Carvery in Cleadon, South Tyneside, where a phantom coach and horses was seen on Christmas Eve many years ago. (Courtesy of Mike Hallowell, Thunderbird Craft and Media)

pub is inscribed with a date of 1675. However, there is evidence that may suggest that an earlier building – also an inn – stood on the site prior to this building. This earlier alehouse may date back as far as the English Civil War.

The Toby Carvery has a wonderful, cosy atmosphere; however, it also has a reputation for being haunted. In 2001 Mike Hallowell was shown around the pub by the landlord, who told him many interesting ghost tales attached to the place. One story in particular caught my attention …

In one of the rooms, which is now used for storage, it appears that a member of staff happened to take a momentary glance out of the window onto the avenue outside and was flabbergasted to see a phantom coach and horses silently glide by.

A customer at the Toby Carvery told Mike a similar story, alleging that his cousin had seen another coach and horses (or

A phantom coach and horses glided silently past.

perhaps it was the same one as the aforementioned coach and four) pull up next to the Toby Carvery one Christmas Eve, before promptly pulling away again and riding off into the distance.

THE WHITE LADY OF CROOK HALL, DURHAM

Just north of Durham City lies the enchanting Crook Hall. It is a short walk from the city centre and stands in majestic surroundings next to the River Wear. This thirteenth-century house provides a dramatic and atmospheric backdrop to its stunning gardens, making it a place of total serenity and extreme beauty.

The Hall was originally built on land that once belonged to Sidgate Manor and was named after Peter Croke, who owned the land back in the early fourteenth century. Nowadays the Hall is the home of the Bell family, who open the house and gardens to the public so that everyone can experience its natural charm and grandeur.

The building has three sections which date from three different periods. The medieval hall was built around 1208, although the solar wing, by all accounts, has long disappeared. The hall, with

An atmospheric shot of a lamp on the walls of the enchanting Crook Hall, Durham City.

its tall stone walls and high roof, provides a magnificent taste of medieval life. Next we have the Jacobean manor house, which was built in 1671. Complete with a circular turret and old-world furniture, combined with the smell of the crackling wood on the open fire, this section of the Hall really does take the visitor back in time. Then we have the Georgian house. Towering three storeys high and adorned with climbing ivy, this section of the house was built by Henry Hopper of the Hopper family of Shincliffe when they purchased the property in 1736.

The house is accompanied by five acres of land with an abundance of beautifully cultivated themed gardens, such as the Shakespeare Garden, which is full of plants that would have been around in the days of the great man himself. Other gardens include the Secret Garden, the Georgian Walled Garden, the Silver and White Garden, the Woodland and Solar Wing Garden, the Cathedral Garden and many more. Decked out with plants and trees including roses, magnolia, azalias, lilac, cherry, plum and apple trees, rhododendrons, hedging, ferns, grapevines and a variety of vegetables, these gardens have been described by gardener and television presenter Alan Titchmarsh as 'a tapestry of colourful blooms', and they are a wonder to behold, no matter what time of the year you chose to visit. There is also a Moat Pool, a pond, and a fantastic maze in the meadow close to the main entrance – brilliant for adults and children alike. But where are the ghosts, I hear you ask.

Well, back in 1463, Cuthbert Billingham inherited Crook Hall and eventually left it to his grandson, John, after his death in or around 1508. Cuthbert Billingham had a niece, and she is the woman thought to be the resident ghost of Crook Hall. Known as the White Lady, she has been observed by many folk as she silently meanders through the house. The ghost of Crook Hall has been well known for many years now and her presence has stirred up much interest within the local paranormal community. Her ghost is seen every now and again, but more often than not, she is felt. The best chance to see the White Lady – in full apparitional form, I am told – is on St Thomas's Eve (20 December) each year. On that particular date, five days before Christmas, she is said to silently float down the ancient wooden staircase that is housed in the circular turret of the Jacobean manor house, her last recorded sighting being not that long ago.

During my visit there, I met Crook Hall's owners, Maggie and Keith Bell, and spoke to them in great detail about their ghost. Keith then took me on a tour of the house and showed me exactly where in the property the ghost is seen, including the area on the old stairwell. He then diverted my attention to a notice on the wall next to where the old stairwell is situated that tells the visitor all about the White Lady. With kind permission from Keith and Maggie, I am able to reproduce the notice:

These ancient stairs, perhaps the oldest in County Durham, are haunted by the White Lady. She was the Niece of Cuthbert Billingham, who inherited Crook Hall. He quarrelled with the citizens of Durham and in his rage, cut off their water supply. There have been numerous

Crook Hall viewed from the bottom of one of their many wonderful gardens.

The ancient stairwell in Crook Hall, down which the resident phantom can be seen floating on St Thomas Eve – December 20.

sightings of the White Lady over the centuries. She is usually said to glide silently and gently down the stairs, although on one occasion, she was reported to thoroughly alarm guests who had been invited to Crook Hall for a ball by a rather more dramatic appearance. A banquet had been laid out in the medieval hall, but as the guests moved into the Screen's Passage, they heard a soft rustle followed by a loud crash. When they looked into the hall they found that the tables had been overturned, destroying the banquet. A further rustle and a glimpse of a white figure convinced them that this was the work of the White lady.

One wonders if the banquet was a Christmas banquet? I wouldn't be surprised if it was. A wonderful anecdote of the Crook Hall ghost to say the least, but one wonders why she chose to ruin the party, after all, she is usually such a benign soul. I have recounted this tale in a lot more detail in my book *Haunted Durham* (The History Press, 2010) which, incidentally, includes my own personal experience of a 'strange happening' during my visit there … but, because this ghost has most certainly got a Christmas connection, I feel it also has a rightful place within these pages too. I must now personally thank Keith and Maggie Bell, to whom we all owe our sincere thanks for keeping the wonderful spirit of Crook Hall well and truly alive for us all to see and enjoy. Long may she walk its ancient passages and halls.

THE HAND OF GLORY, SCOTCH CORNER, NORTH YORKSHIRE

The Old Spital Inn was situated near Scotch Corner in North Yorkshire. The pub, which is now long gone, was, by all accounts, a spit and sawdust kind of place where you would not want to spend the night, especially if you were travelling alone. The ghost tale that is attached to the old pub, and indeed, the area itself, is an eerie one and is aptly named the 'hand of glory'.

One Christmas, back in the 1700s, a fierce winter storm closed in on the area known as Scotch Corner. The storm lasted for days on end, with temperatures almost matching those in the Antarctic, and blizzards so thick one could barley tolerate being outside for more that five minutes at a time. The Old Spital Inn was a lot less busy than it would have been as local people dared not venture out from their homes during the storm; nevertheless, the bedrooms were all fully occupied by guests who had arrived before the storm. Now, the guests were literally snowed in and unable to leave.

After spending a night in the establishment's bar – having nothing else better to do – the guests drank their remaining pints of ale and then made their way back to their rooms to sleep off their drunken stupors. After the bar had been closed up, and everyone was fast asleep in their beds, the landlord of the inn and his family retired to their quarters for a well-deserved rest. The only individual left downstairs at this point was the cook. She was left to tidy up the premises and generally make things 'all well and good' for the next day. After finishing her duties, she sat down by the roaring fire in the kitchen with a nightcap and warmed herself in front of the orange-red flames that danced and crackled in the huge fireplace.

Sitting there relaxing, her eyes began to slowly close. Suddenly, there came a ferocious banging from the front door of the inn. She rose with a start, and rushed to see who on earth could be knocking at such a late hour, and in such treacherous conditions too. When she opened the huge oak door, she was astonished to see before her an elderly lady, standing shivering and trembling in the icy-winds. It was obvious to the cook that this old woman was in dire need of some help, so without further-ado, she brought her inside the premises and wrapped her up in a thick blanket. Frozen through, the old lady explained that she was a homeless soul and needed somewhere to sleep for the night.

The cook informed her that the inn was full, but, being a kindly soul, she provided a space in the kitchen for her and gave her blankets to lie on so that she could spend the night near the roaring fire. After the makeshift bed was prepared, the cook bade the woman goodnight and began to prepare to turn in herself. As she was about to leave the kitchen to venture to her own room, she noticed something rather strange. Under the old woman's clothes she noticed that she had on a pair of man's trousers. After pulling the door to, leaving a small gap between the door and its frame, she suspiciously peeked through the slight gap to see what the old woman would do next.

It seems the frail and frozen old lady was not what she appeared to be. She was, in fact, a man. The cook watched in horror as this man crawled across the floor of the kitchen until he reached the huge oak table. There, he reached into his inside pocket and pulled out a withered and almost skeletal human hand. The cook was now frightened out of her wits, but, very much intrigued by what was going on, she kept watching. The impostor precariously balanced the grim relic upon a candlestick and then produced a small bottle. He removed its cork and poured the contents onto the tip of each finger. Then he lit each finger one by one. Four fingers were now burning away furiously, but the fifth digit would not light.

The cook realised that the lighted fingers on the hand were a symbol of how many permanent residents of the inn were fast asleep. The reason the fifth digit on the hand had not lit was because the cook was still awake! The cook ran upstairs to awaken the innkeeper and his family, but all attempts to shake them from their slumbers proved fruitless. It seems that the magic spell that the imposter had utilised proved too good. The cook realised that as long as the fingers were burning on the 'hand of glory' those affected by its spell would stay asleep. They would not wake until the flames were extinguished.

By now the villain had opened the inn door and let in his gang of vagabonds. They busied themselves ransacking the place and stealing just about everything they could get their hands on. The cook knew that the only way to break the spell was to put out

An artist's illustration of a glowing 'Hand of Glory'. (Drew Bartley)

the flaming fingers of the hand. She had remembered that an old wives' tale once stipulated that 'to put out demon flames one must use "blue"'. Blue, for those who don't know, is an expression for the use of 'skimmed milk'.

By now the robbers had left the kitchen area and the burning hand was unattended. This was her chance. She rushed into the kitchen frantically looking around for a jug of milk. Much to her dismay, she could not locate it. In a desperate attempt, she picked up a jug of ale and cast it over the flames, the fires still burned. Then she quickly filled a pail of water and threw it on to the hand, but still the flames continued to burn relentlessly. By now she was in a complete state and it would only be another minute or two before the robbers would return.

Once again, she glanced around the room and finally spotted a pan of skimmed milk. She picked it up and hurled it across the room. The milk landed on the hand and put out the flames in an instant. At that point everyone in the inn woke up and quickly made their way downstairs to see what was going on. The robbers were caught red-handed and were subsequently arrested. By first light they were all in jail awaiting certain death. The grim relic, the hand of glory, was taken away and buried underneath the local gibbet post.

This is a bizarre story, yet it was taken very seriously by the locals who, for many years after the event, swore on oath it was true. But is there really any truth in the legend? Well, in the mid-fifteenth century it was believed that the preserved left hand of a hanged man – which was known as a 'hand of glory' – could send people in the close vicinity to sleep if the fingers were lit up like a candles. It is thought that the hand would have to be soaked in a number of substances. Perhaps this was what the would-be-robber poured down the fingertips before setting fire to the fingers? Two of the substances thought to have been used are vervain and mandrake – both of which have amazing anaesthetic qualities and can put you to sleep in a matter of minutes. So, there may be some scientific basis behind the idea, as fumes from these two plants could have sent the residents of the Old Spital Inn into a deep slumber. However, keeping the slumbering residents fast asleep in the rooms upstairs, well, I am not too sure.

The Old Spital Inn is now long gone now, but some folk suggest that the Bowes Moor Hotel, which is located midway across the A66 from Scotch Corner, is the actual building that was once known as the Old Spital Inn. Others suggest that the Bowes Moor Hotel was built upon the foundations of the original Spital Inn. Whatever the case, the hand of glory legend lives on.

In Whitby Museum one particular exhibit has created mass interest and is possibly the most popular piece in the museum. It

The Bowes Moor Hotel, which stands on the A66 between Scotch Corner in North Yorkshire and Penrith in Cumbria. It is said to have been built on the same site as the Old Spital Inn.

is, of course, a hand of glory. Is it the hand from Scotch Corner and the Old Spital Inn? No one knows for sure. One thing is certain though; when you see it through its glass case, it certainly sends a shiver down your spine. If you are ever in Whitby and have time on your hands (pardon the pun), I would suggest you pop in and take a look at it.

KIRKSTONE PASS INN, CUMBRIA

The desolate and windswept pub known as the Kirkstone Pass Inn is located on Patterdale Road, on the Kirkstone Pass, near Ambleside in the picturesque Lake District. The inn dates mainly from around the seventeenth century, although some parts of the building go back to the fifteenth. The inn is one of Cumbria's highest public houses, standing at 1,489ft above sea level. The views you get from this area are spectacular, with the

Lakeland mountainous ranges and untamed wilderness reaching out far before you in almost every direction. The acclaimed poet, William Wordsworth (1770–1850) visited the inn during many of his Lakeland adventures and penned the line 'who comes not hither ne'er shall know how beautiful the world below'.

The Kirkstone Pass Inn was formerly known as the Travellers Rest, which was an apt name, for many weary travellers and visitors to the area would stop off here to rest their tired legs and take in some much needed refreshment. Of course, being the ancient building that it is, it is not surprising to hear that this public house has not just retained its charm and character, but, by all accounts, a few of its former patrons too – in the form of resident ghosts.

Many people over the years have reported 'strange occurrences' within the walls of this old drinking den, including much violent poltergeist-like activity. Doors are said to open and close on their own, glasses are thrown from behind the bar and staff and visitors alike often feel an eerie presence. These disturbances are put down to two alleged ghosts. The first is that of a lost hiker who, for whatever reason, decided to vent his aggression in this old building, and the other is a grey lady.

Some folk suggest that these two ghosts are not responsible for this at all, and blame a phantom child named Neville. He is thought to be responsible for the movement of furniture and picture frames. Neville, according to Richard Jones in his book *Haunted Inns of Britain and Ireland*, was alleged to have been killed outside the inn when he was run over by a coach and horses.

The area outside the inn is reputedly haunted too. Nearby, there is a tree that is known as the 'hangman's tree' – no prizes for guessing what happened there in days gone by. Stories persist of a harrowing spectral form seen around the hangman's tree. The spectre is thought to be that of a former innkeeper from the 1700s, who was accused of brutally murdering his children after they disappeared from the inn without any warning.

The final ghost – the one that ties the Kirkstone Pass Inn to the theme of this book – is the ghost of Ruth, who haunts the area every Christmas time; around the anniversary of her tragic death. The story goes that, one inclement night, she decided to set off with her newborn baby into the darkness to see her ill father. During her efforts to reach her father's house, she was caught up in a winter blizzard. The blizzard became so severe she began to worry about her child. She took off some of her garments and wrapped the baby up so the child would be warm.

Ruth then forced her way forwards, heading on into the driving snow, eventually succumbing to it. Freezing cold, she dropped to the ground. It was not long before Ruth died of exposure, but happily the baby survived and was found soon after. Ruth's sad ghost is said to be seen around Christmas at the dead of night as she endlessly searches the area in vain looking for her beloved child.

An artist's impression of Ruth and her child as she sets off to see her sick father. She is thought to haunt the road near the Kirkstone Pass Inn in the Lake District. (Julie Olley)

THE SKULLS OF CALGARTH HALL, LAKE WINDERMERE, CUMBRIA

Calgarth Hall stands imposingly on the shore of Lake Windermere, and is one of the oldest buildings in the surrounding area. Allegedly, the manor house was once subjected to a haunting connected to the unjust killing of two innocent people.

Kraster Cook and his wife Dorothy lived on an area of land which was very much sought after by one of the locals, a man named Myles Phillipson. By all accounts, Pillipson was a wealthy, influential man who was used to getting his own way. However, the Cooks refused to sell him their land and no amount of money or persuasion would convince them to part with their precious house. Phillipson wanted the land to build upon. He had designs to build a grandiose manor house and nothing would stop him in his venture ... nothing.

Christmas time – the season of good will to all men – was approaching and Phillipson had hatched a plan. He turned up out of the blue at the Cooks' house claiming that he wanted to make piece with them and forget their differences. He told them that he had no more fancy ideas about 'gaining the land' and that they had nothing more to worry about. During his impromptu visit, he also invited the Cooks to his house for 'Christmas Dinner', to which Kraster and Dorothy reluctantly accepted. They had a sneaky suspicion that Phillipson was up to no good; perhaps they should have listened to their 'gut feelings', as they turned out to be chillingly correct.

The Cooks turned up on Christmas Day at Phillipson's house and were pleasantly surprised at how courteous and friendly their host and the other guests were. However, as they felt out of place amongst so many affluent people, they stayed only a short while before thanking their host and leaving. Kraster and Dorothy Cook's suspicions about Phillipson's intentions were soon confirmed when the following day (Boxing Day) a troop of soldiers turned up at their home and arrested them. After carrying out a search of the premises, they just happened to 'find' a silver bowl that had been on display during the party at Phillipson's house on Christmas Day. The insinuation, of course, was that the Cooks had stolen the silver bowl during the Christmas gathering.

The astonished couple were carted off to prison whereupon, after a week in captivity, they were put on trial. Of course, all the witnesses were the associates of Phillipson and they testified against the Cooks – the couple never stood a chance. They were found guilty of theft and sentenced to hang. Prior to their unjust execution, and out of desperation, Dorothy Cook lost her temper and flew off into a rage. She raised her hand, pointed at Phillipson and, through gritted teeth, uttered a chilling curse:

Watch out for yourself, Master Phillipson! You might think you have done a fine thing, but that tiny scrap of land you lust for will prove to be the dearest a Phillipson has ever bought or pinched. Neither you nor your breed will ever prosper on it, and whatever plan or scheme you take up will wither in your hand. Whatever cause you set your arm to will always a loser be. The time will come when no Phillipson will own so much as an inch of land, and while Calgarth walls stand, we will haunt them night and day. You will never be rid of us!

The Cooks were hanged by their necks until they were dead. Even before the bodies of Kraster and Dorothy Cook were taken down from the gallows, work had begun on Phillipson's new and lavish home. Their little cottage was torn down before their bodies were even cold. A magnificent new dwelling of infinitely grander proportions was planned. Phillipson had got his way, as usual, but it wouldn't be long before he regretted his actions; the Cooks were, quite literally, coming back to haunt him.

Once the house was built and Phillipson had moved in, the paranormal activity began. Doors would slam shut, furniture

Kraster and Dorothy Cook hanging by their necks after being framed for theft.

moved around when no one was near it, and chilling screams reverberated through the residence, keeping Phillipson awake almost every night. However, the most harrowing event was the discovery of two grinning skulls, found resting on a banister rail. The skulls, ironically, were discovered on Christmas Day – one year to the day since Phillipson had set up the Cooks so that he could take their land.

A terrified Phillipson ordered the skulls to be destroyed. But, after they had been disposed of, they were found back in the house in the same spot where they were originally found grinning macabrely. Phillipson was not so smug now. He even had the skulls weighed down and thrown into Lake Windermere, but, yet again, they found their way back into

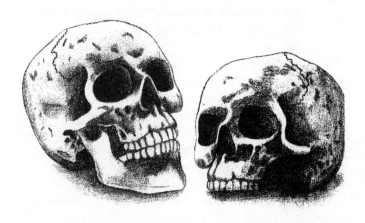

An artist's impression of two grinning skulls just like those of Kraster and Dorothy Cook who haunted Calgarth Hall. (Julie Olley)

the house intact. Whatever he did to try and rid the household of Kraster and Dorothy Cook's ghastly skulls … they kept on returning. Eventually, he accepted the fact that he could not get rid of them, and left them where they were found in the house, on the banister rail. Dorothy's prophecy had come true – Phillipson would never be rid of them. Phillipson now knew for sure that this was the work of the Cooks. They had come back to haunt him, with a tormenting vengeance. The two skulls remained inside Calgarth Hall, grinning menacingly at Phillipson each time he walked past them. In fact, the Cooks haunted the house – and Phillipson – until the day he died, as they said they would.

THE SCHOONER HOTEL, NORTHUMBERLAND, 25 DECEMBER 1806

The Schooner Hotel is allegedly one the UK's most haunted hotels. This seventeenth-century coaching inn is reputed to have over sixty ghosts including a spirit called William, who is said to have murdered his family where rooms 28, 29 and 30 are now situated. This area is the oldest section of the hotel and at one time was one big living area. Split into three many years ago, all three of these rooms reputedly have their fair share of paranormal activity.

The ghost of Parson John is said to meander the ground floor of the hotel in the month of September. Killed accidentally while opening a cask of his own special brew ale, the ghost is said to be seen holding the tap high above his head for all to see. The tap had 'fired off' and hit him on the head, so the story goes, but recently I was informed by a former employee of the hotel that the ghost of Parson John was nothing more than an elaborate hoax to try and 'drum up business' for the hotel, which, at that time, was not doing too well.

I, however, have investigated the building on nearly fifteen occasions now and can testify to the fact that strange things do indeed go on there. I have personally seen doors open slowly, before slamming closed very loudly, I have heard footsteps in corridors when no one else was with me, I have found previously locked doors to be open (when I was the only person with the key) and have witnessed objects moving on their own.

The Christmas story I wish to relate to you from this wonderful old establishment dates back to 1806. It was Christmas Day when Alnmouth witnessed one of its worst storms in history. In fact, the storm was so severe it changed the actual course of the river. As the rain lashed down and the wind howled outside, a small family huddled inside, around a huge burning fire in what is now the hotel's 'Chase Bar', the youngest

The Schooner Hotel in Alnmouth, Northumberland, is said to be haunted by the ghost of a young girl who was killed on Christmas Day in the Chase Bar in 1806.

girl sleeping on her mother's knee. They were eagerly awaiting the return of the head of their family – a devoted husband and father who was out in the North Sea trawling the stormy waters in search of fish. Suddenly, the door to the inn burst open, allowing the treacherous wind and rain to blow furiously inside. A number of fishermen entered the inn carrying a body. It was the corpse of the husband. He had been killed while out at sea. The mother quickly rose to her feet with her hands over her mouth, horrified at the sight of her dead husband. As she stood, her daughter, who had been sleeping on her lap, fell into the roaring fire, hitting her heard upon the hearth in the process. She was immediately pulled from the flames by her family but she was badly burned and subsequently died of her injuries. She was just six years old.

Her ghost has been seen and heard in the hotel's Chase Bar. One witness said that while she was sitting in the restaurant area of the hotel, she heard the sound of a young girl coming from around the corner. We don't know if the sounds that she heard were sounds of laughter or the sound of sobbing, but, knowing the bar was empty, she decided to venture around and have a look. As she turned the corner – still hearing the girl – she was astonished to find the room completely empty. Not only that, but as soon as she turned the corner and ventured into the room, the noise of the girl immediately ceased, leaving an eerie silence in which one could hear a pin drop.

Another witness claimed to have seen a young girl disappear in front of her eyes while she was having a drink in the bar. The girl, it is said, silently ran into the bar area from around the corner, whereupon she stopped dead in the room. She glanced up at the woman and then vanished into thin air, right in front of her.

THE SCOTIA HOTEL, SOUTH SHIELDS

Another phantom who makes his presence known at Christmas time is 'Tommy the Cellerman', who haunts the Scotia Hotel, a quaint little old pub that sits more or less in the centre of South Shields' busy shopping precinct, on King Street. This one-time spit and sawdust alehouse became so popular with the South Shields locals that an extension had to be built. Eventually, due to more and more people drinking there, the alehouse was completely demolished and a much larger pub took its place. This wonderful 'Victorian Long Bar' still does a rip-roaring trade, even after many years of business.

Tommy the Cellarman was said by some to have died on the premises of the Scotia Hotel back in the mid-1970s, although this is not certain. What is certain is that Tommy walked with a distinct limp, and was quite often seen hobbling around the pub with his trusty old walking stick. After his death, staff at the pub often reported hearing the shuffle of footsteps accompanied by the tap, tap, tap of a walking stick.

The Scotia Hotel in South Shields, Tyne and Wear. (Courtesy of Mike Hallowell, Thunderbird Craft and Media)

What makes the staff believe this is the ghost of Tommy is the fact that these eerie sounds are heard as they make their way up and down the cellar steps, the steps which Tommy used almost everyday while he was alive. It is said that a former landlady once took a photograph of some staff members one Christmas and, when the picture was developed, there was Tommy the Cellarman alongside everyone else, bold as brass. Why he should make his appearance at Christmas is anyones guess. Perhaps Christmas was his favourite time of year, and he simply wanted to join in with the seasonal festivities. I have attempted to track down this elusive photograph, but so far my efforts have sadly proved fruitless.

Tommy can still be heard on occasions as he goes about his usual business – up and down the cellar stairs – tap, tap, tapping as he goes. It seems that Tommy has no plans to leave the pub anytime soon, so who knows, maybe this Christmas, or perhaps the next, he might show up in another festive photo as the staff and patrons celebrate the Yuletide.

THE STOGURSEY MONKS OF BRIDGWATER, SOMERSET

An article in the *Somerset Herald*, dated 27 February 1927, states that the area known as Monkswood in the village of Stogursey was once subjected to a haunting. A man going by the initials of B.T. stated that, 'I have brought to memory something I had not thought of for the past forty or fifty years.'

B.T. goes on to explain that he remembers from his boyhood the ghost story attached to that area and states that any youngsters that happened to pass an area known as Monkswood, when it was getting 'dimpsy' (one presume he means dark), had a very real chance of seeing the ghosts. He goes on to mention that one day, near this area, a coach and pair had a terrible accident. The coach belonged to one F.W. Meade-King and was being driven by a local coachman named Mr Tremlet. Mr Tremlet, declared that the accident was no fault of his own and stated that one horse 'saw something', resulting in it becoming very frightened and knocking the other horse over. A roundhouse at the local priory, he also claimed, had an underground tunnel that led to the nearby castle. This was the area where the ghosts would 'take shelter' during bad weather.

This first letter prompted the response of another reader, dated 6 March 1927, who remained anonymous, to recall his memories of growing up in Stogursey:

As an old Stogursey boy I can well remember the accident to the vicar's carriage at Monkton Wells owing to one of the horses seeing a ghost. As mentioned by 'B.T.' in last weeks *Herald*. As regards to the ghost of a monk recently seen in the Roundhouse, well many years ago the ghost of a monk used to be seen disappearing towards the quarry adjoining Monks Wood. I was once told by a very old workman, who had worked at the Priory in his younger days, that on Christmas Eve at midnight the monks could be seen walking down the steps leading from the upper room of the old Roundhouse, and making their way towards the priory barn.

An artist's impresstion of the precession of the Stogursey Monks, who can be seen at midnight on Christmas Eve in an area known as 'Monkswood'. (Drew Bartley)

So, why do the monks haunt this area? Well, it has been suggested that the Round House was known as a 'counting house' during the monk's occupation of the priory, and by all accounts it had been 'tampered with' in some way. Unfortunately, my source does not go into details as to what happened there, but categorically states that, 'As if to protest this sacrilege, the ghosts of the monks have taken to haunt.'

THE BATTLE OF EDGEHILL, WARWICKSHIRE

On 23 October 1642 the Battle of Edgehill took place in Warwickshire. Twenty-four thousand men fought against each other, with many men perishing on the battlefield. The ironic thing is that that particular battle had no victors, with both armies eventually making off in their respective directions after camping out on the battlefield after the fight. The battle was fought between Charles I – who had 11,000 men – and the Earl of Essex – who had 13,000 men – on the sloped banks of Edgehill over-looking the Avon Valley, south of Warwick, and it marked the onset of the English Civil War.

Sixty-two days after the battle, on Christmas Eve, the sounds of battle cries, galloping and neighing horses, and the thud of far-off drums being beaten were heard by three wandering shepherds and many other locals. Then, out of the blue, the two armies appeared in phantom form in the skies over Edgehill, battling out once more the fight that had recently occurred there. This spectral scene was reported to have lasted for many hours before it slowly faded into the ether, leaving the skies over Edgehill silent once more.

Those who saw the spectral forms on 24 December 1642 rushed off to sign declarations to bear witness to what they had seen. This resulted in many people gathering at the site the following night to see if the phantom soldiers would return once more. December 25 1642 saw the Battle of Edgehill being played out once more in spectral form, giving many more people a chance to see, and verify for themselves, these ghastly visions of brutal warfare. Many people continued to return to the site to see for themselves what everyone was by now talking about but for the next four of five days the vision failed to appear. It was almost a week later (some suggest 31 December) when the ghost armies appeared once more, much to the delight of those who were awaiting them. Interestingly, when King Charles I heard about the visions, he sent some of his men to see the spectacle. It is reported that a number of these men saw the re-enactment and actually recognised some of their fellow comrades while doing so. They all testified this on oath to Charles I.

The following evening, the phantom soldiers took to the battlefields (or battle skies in this case) for one last time before fading away into the atmosphere, never to be seen again. However, it is said that for many years after the Battle of Edgehill, on 23 October, the sounds of the battle could be heard as though it was

The phantom battle over the skies of Edgehill in Warwickshire. Probably one of the most famous accounts of Christmas ghosts on record. (Trevor Yorke)

being played out yet again, only this time no visions appeared. Peter Underwood comments in his book *The A-Z of British Ghosts* that within the space of twelve months of the battle being fought, a small pamphlet was published that described the spectral re-enactment of the armies that fought each other on that fateful day back in 1642. It is thanks to these writings that the story of Edgehill remains in our modern-day literature, and is a testament to the fact that these types of visions do indeed occur.

Why the phantom battle was seen over two nights at Christmas and another two nights a week later and not on the anniversary of the actual battle like the auditory phenomenon was, I guess we will never know for sure.

THE CHRISTMAS GIFT … OF LIFE, TAUNTON, SOMERSET

A newspaper clipping from the *Somerset County Herald*, dated 18 December 1948, carried a fascinating story of kindness, love, sadness, death and joy. This tale of a friendly and warm presence really epitomises the 'Christmas ghost'.

It was 1730, and one Henry Transom MA arrived in Taunton, Somerset, to begin work at Taunton Grammar School. His specialised subject was 'Classics'. Henry Transom was a single man aged forty, and rented a number of rooms in a large Tudor-style house in East Street in the town. He was a devout Christian and regularly attended services at his local church, St Mary's.

Farmers at this time complained that they could not sell their grain due to the lack of demand so the government stepped in with a new, but not so clever initiative. They suggested that the farmers having trouble selling on their grain should begin to brew and manufacture their own alcohol – especially Gin – and pledged to cancel all the taxes on its production, and the need for a licence to sell it. Now, people couldn't get enough of their share of the grain. It had gone from one extreme to the other. Of course it wasn't just the quality beverage-makers making the drink; a great deal of cheap, crude and very badly made alcohol was also produced. Many people were made ill with the 'dodgy grog' and health took a serious turn for the worse. Dirty streets, insanitary houses and rotten drinking water helped to pave the way for a widespread outbreak of small-pox and cholera. The death rate, especially in young children, was high.

Henry Transom noticed all of this occurring, and it bothered him. Being the kind of man he was, he decided to try and help the poor and needy. He was inspired by the Greek physicians of ancient history who gave freely to the poor. These Greek healers, who employed the Hippocratic concept of therapeutics, used means such as diets and medicinal herbs, which, it was thought, attained a high level of positive results. This was in stark contrast to the early eighteenth-century methods of treatment such as using bleedings and drugs.

He was prompted into action one night when he came across a sentence in the Bible which read, 'I was sick, and ye visited me'. He pondered long and hard over the sentence, which seemed to 'light up' as his eyes fell across pages. From that point he made regular gifts and donations to his local infirmary – which included seven parcels of delicacies being sent to the convalescents every Christmas. His good deeds won him a place in the hearts of the poorest of people. It was also his goal to build a hospital in Taunton; somewhere for the sick to go. He visited the poor and unwell all over the community, taking gifts and offering prayers for them. In half the cases, it is said, he believed that 'people needed prayers more that they needed pills', and 'meditation, more than they needed medication'. In 1758, after many years of tending to his people, and not realising his dream of the local hospital, he contracted small-pox and sadly died.

Transom's close friends and colleagues duly paid their homage to him after his death, but noticed something rather odd while visiting his former rented accommodation on East Street. 'It had seemed,' they said, 'that even after his death, his very essence, his very being, had soaked into the surrounding walls. The warmth of his personality seemed to survive in the rooms,' they claimed.

Forty-three years passed and in 1801 a corn merchant named George Marshall purchased the property, which included Transom's former rented rooms. George had a son, an only child, who attended the Grammar School in Taunton. His bedroom was the same one which once housed Transom all those years ago and, coincidentally, he too was called Henry. Some time after moving into the new house, the night before Christmas, Henry became ill. He had contracted pneumonia, so his father had quickly contacted a local nurse, who immediately came to the young boy's aid. Arriving at the house on Christmas Eve, she hurriedly ran upstairs into the boy's room to tend to him.

While upstairs, the nurse experienced what she described as 'two extraordinary phenomena' happening. She saw a luminous patch mysteriously appear on the bedroom wall in which she saw the distinct outline of a rod and serpent (symbols that were often associated with the Greek physicians). Then, from out of nowhere, appeared a man's figure across the room. It glided silently past her before placing its hand on to the sick boy's forehead. A man's voice then uttered, 'I was sick, and ye visited me', before the figure stood upright, and then walked off through the wall. The nurse claimed that the room felt as though it was filled with a 'gracious presence' and reported that, from that point on, young Henry began his miraculous road to recovery; a very welcome Christmas gift, to say the least.

The local nurse was contacted.

An artist's impression of the phantom thought to be Henry Transom, who saved Henry Marshall's life as he was dying in his bed from pneumonia. (Courtesy of Mike Hallowell, Thunderbird Craft and Media)

Those that knew Transom believed that it was his spirit which had came back to save the life of young Henry, continuing his good work in the afterlife.

Things were not the same in that house from that point. A barrage of weird occurrences were documented, indicating that Transom was indeed still there, making his presence known. For example, a roll of bandages appeared from nowhere one day. On another occasion the family Bible was found open at Matthew, chapter 25, on the page where the sentence, 'I was sick, and ye visited me' occurs. Pencil markings began to appear on the walls from time to time, with one scribbling in particular reading the word *Iatros*, the Greek word for physician. All these incidences supported the idea that Transom was back; but why?

In 1810 work began on the Taunton and Somerset Hospital, resulting in immense progression being made in regard to the health and care of the people of Taunton and Somerset. From the moment the foundation stone was laid on April 11, the spirit of Henry Transom was laid too. No more accounts of 'odd happenings' were reported at the house in East Street and all fell quiet in Taunton. Henry Transom was evidently so passionate about seeing his much-wanted hospital built that he had to come back from beyond the grave to see it.

THE GHOST GIRL OF WESTOE, SOUTH TYNESIDE

During my research into ghosts associated with the festive season, I happened to stumble upon a Christmas Ghost story which has to be one of the most heartbreaking tales I have ever heard and allegedly resulted in one of South Tyneside's most unhappy ghosts.

A colleague, Violet, recalled a tale that was told to her by her mother, who in turn had the story told to her by her mother. This is how the classic ghost story survives through the years; but having said that, it is also how the ghost story can become distorted and potentially embellished, so we must be careful here.

Dating back at least to the mid-to-late nineteenth century, this tale, which is quite well known by the Westoe folk in South Tyneside, begins one Christmas Eve when a young lady, seemingly a housemaid or a domestic worker, had a 'night out'.

She worked in one of the 'big houses' at Westoe and, it seems, was instructed by her master not to partake in local Christmas festivities. However, these strict instructions were blatantly disregarded by the servant girl and she proceeded to put on her 'glad rags' and 'hit the town'. Like most folk, she wanted to go out and celebrate the festive season with friends. She quietly crept out of her master's residence and made her way to one of the local inns. Not knowing the exact year, it's difficult to say just where she may have ended up, but in all probability it would have been the Westoe Tavern, or the now long-demolished Mariner's Arms. However, she may have journeyed a little farther and downed a few at the Vigilant Inn or the Ship Inn at Harton Village nearby.

Westoe village, South Tyneside.

After her night out at the inn, she merrily made her way back to her master's house and tried to gain access. However, she was met by her master who was furious with her. Not only did he seriously reprimand her for refusing to comply with his orders, but he also told the girl never to darken his door again. He closed the door and locked it behind him, leaving her out in the cold. Now she was in big trouble, for not only was the master's house her place of employment, it was also where she lived.

It was a bitterly cold winter's night and thick snow had fallen across the land. The servant girl had nowhere to go, so she began banging on the doors and windows of her master's house, pleading with him to forgive her and let her back in, but he refused. In desperation, she began banging on the doors of the other houses in the neighbourhood, but to no avail. The only thing she was met with was the twitching of the curtains at the windows, and the occasional individual peering from inside the warm and cosy abodes. All she could do now was attempt to find some shelter for

The old road that runs down by the 'Westoe Pub'. The hollow tree that the ghost girl of Westoe was thought to have died in is now sadly long gone, but it was thought to have stood at the foot of this lane.

the night. Frantically looking around, she spotted a large hollow tree, so she hurriedly scrambled over to it. As she climbed into the hollow, she sobbed uncontrollably. She curled herself up in a ball, and tried to keep warm. The following morning she was found, still inside the tree, frozen to death. My colleague tells me that the ghost of the young woman has been seen in Westoe village on Christmas Eve, still searching desperately for shelter.

I wanted to know more about this sad tale so I contacted Mike Hallowell; for the last twelve years Mike has penned a weekly spooky column called WraithScape (formerly Bizarre) in the *Shields Gazette*. He was very much intrigued when I asked him about the tale but admitted that he knew nothing about it. However, Mike did make a suggestion. With the information I had collated, he would write the story up in his column and, at the same time, make an appeal to the good folk of Westoe – or anywhere else for that matter – to contact me if they could shed any light upon the tale.

What was the servant's name? Where exactly did she work? Where was she from? Did she really exist? Could we trace anyone who had actually seen her ghost? The piece went in the paper on Thursday, 28 January 2010 and only one response was received thereafter. In a letter addressed to Mike Hallowell, a lady claimed that 200 yards down the lane that runs next to the Westoe public house stood a tree trunk that had been filled in with black pitch. Rumour had it that someone had been murdered and then stuffed into the hollow tree: she wondered if this was, or could have been, the same girl. The plot, it seems, begins to thicken! Further investigations are being carried out by both Mike and myself in order to try and get to the bottom of the ghost girl of Westoe – watch this space.

An illustration of the cold and lonely girl as she hides in a hollow tree on Christmas Eve to shelter from the ice-cold night. It was here where she died and her ghost is reputed to haunt the area. (Courtesy of Mike Hallowell, Thunderbird Craft and Media)

THE *BETSY JANE*

Upon perusing the Christmas edition of *Paranormal Magazine*, I discovered an article dedicated to ghostly goings on around Christmas time which had been written and submitted by John Stoker. One story in particular caught my eye and I contacted John to ask him if I could re-print the story – entitled, 'On Christmas Day in the Morning' – and he very kindly obliged.

In the days of the slave trade the *Betsy Jane* was returning to England having sold its human cargo and was approaching the Solway Firth. It was Christmas Eve and the crew could hear the church bells on the shore. The captain was now a wealthy man and boasted that the sounds of coins were sweeter than any church bell. His words were cut short by the sound of shattering timbers as the ship hit the Giltstone Rock. The vessel sank within a few minutes with the loss of the entire crew, leaving no sound but the peal of the church bells of Whitehaven. The following

A photograph of a ghost ship, just like the ship known as the Betsy Jane *that haunts the shores of Whitehaven in Cumbria. (Courtesy of Mike Hallowell, Thunderbird Craft and Media)*

Christmas the *Betsy Jane* was seen again from the shore and has continued her ghostly voyage ever since.

THE RECTOR'S SPECTRE –
ST PETER'S, DORCHESTER

It is said that the Revd Nathaniel Templeman, who was the rector of St Peter's Church in Dorchester, died in 1813 and his body was subsequently buried in the church itself. By all accounts he was a strict member of the clergy and was known to have kept a close eye on his parishioners.

On Christmas Eve the following year two of the church wardens were in the church preparing it for Christmas and decorating the aisles. When they completed their tasks they decided to have a rest and drink a sly glass or two of the communion wine that was being stored in the vestry. As they got comfortable on the wooden pews, they suddenly felt that they were not alone.

Before they had a chance to get even one mouthful of wine, they were confronted by the ghost of Nathaniel Templeman. He thundered his way down the church aisle, hands raised and a displeasing look upon his face. Although it was clear that the rector was shouting and yelling at the men, no sounds emerged – a bit like watching the television with the volume turned off. One man dropped to his knees and began to pray, and the other just simply passed out. The phantom rector then made his way to the altar before disappearing into thin air.

The rector was obviously very much annoyed with the two wardens for stealing the communion wine. Making the point in the way he did ensured that these two opportunists would think twice before helping themselves to Church property again.

The spectre of Revd Nathaniel Templeman, who was seen in St Peter's Church in Dorchester on Christmas Eve in 1814 by two churchwardens. Although the Rector was clearly shouting and yelling at the men, no sounds came from him at all.

Car Crash at Christmas

Many years ago, a couple from South Tyneside went to stay with some of their family in South Africa for the Christmas and New Year period. When they got there, they were told a chilling ghost tale which, by all accounts, was true. The story was relayed to the family on Christmas Eve, days after the actual event.

It was their grandchild who told the story. It appears that he had gone to visit a friend whose parents had decided to go out for an evening drive. Left with the house to themselves, like most teenagers, the two friends had plans for an evening of partying.

However, their plans were short-lived because, shortly after the parents had left, they returned home in a very distressed state.

When the boys asked what was wrong, the two adults wasted no time in explaining what had had occurred. They were out driving when they decided to stop somewhere for a bite to eat, and so headed to a pub they knew that sold good food. This pub was 'out in the sticks' so to speak, so they were forced to drive down an old, deserted country road.

About halfway down the road the couple noticed a woman standing at the roadside. At this point she must have been about 200ft away. The car approached the woman, who was waving at the car, trying to get them to stop. She looked distressed so the couple pulled over to see if they could help in any way. The husband got out from the car and walked around to the distraught lady. He asked what was wrong but the woman could not speak. He asked again, but still no words came from the lady's mouth. He asked one final time and, yet again, she uttered no words. She must be in shock, he thought to himself.

Then the woman pointed towards a copse of trees about 50ft away from them. As he looked in the direction she was pointing he noticed something. Upon taking a closer look he was stunned to see the wreckage of a car that had obviously careered off the road and had crashed into the trees. He told the distraught woman not to worry and rushed back to his car to ask his wife to phone for help. When he returned to find the lady, he was dumbfounded to see that she had vanished from the scene altogether. He stopped and thought for a moment, wondering where she could have got to, but then realised that there was no time to lose; if there were injured people in the car they would need medical assistance, and quickly.

He ran as fast as he could towards the car and, as he approached it from the rear, he could see that there were two seriously injured people in the front seat. He dashed around the front to see if they were still alive but both were slumped forwards and obviously dead. He took hold of the man in the driving seat and sat him back to make sure that he *was* deceased. He then turned his attention to the woman in the passenger seat. As he looked closely at her, he was horrified to see that *she* was the very same woman who had just flagged him down from the roadside moments earlier.

He then heard a faint cry coming from the back of the car and when he looked closer he saw a young baby under the debris. The baby had survived the crash.

The ghost of the recently killed mother, it seems, was still looking after her child – even in death.

This is not the first account of a ghost coming back from the dead to rescue somebody. A similar occurrence happened on the A1 motorway between Morpeth and Berwick-upon-Tweed when the ghost of a back-packer returned from beyond the grave to save the victim of a car crash, a crash that the ghost had inadvertently caused.

THE COWLED MONK OF ST PETER'S, HEREFORD

On 23 December 1926 two policemen were on foot patrol near St Peter's Church in Hereford when they both saw something that frightened them half to death. As they were strolling past the church gate they happened to glance inside towards the church door and see a 'strange, hooded figure dressed in a black cloak'. He drifted silently past the iron railings on the outskirts of the church grounds and disappeared from view.

The two policemen decided to investigate further, just in case it was a burglar, and ventured inside the church grounds. They soon caught sight of the hooded figure once more, but were horrified to then see it drift straight through some locked iron gates and float off towards the porch of the church. Before the two bobbies could react, the figure then floated straight through the locked doors of the church and disappeared from view altogether.

The policemen's account of the ghost of St Peter's spread through Hereford quickly and it was not long before others

Is the hooded-spectre the ghost of a monk?

ventured forth and relayed their own ghost stories; the policemen's encounter was not the first time the hooded figure had been seen. The father of a former organist at the church admitted that he too, had seen the ghost. He had seen the black hooded figure on a few occasions and on one of those occasions it had floated through the same wooden door. He pointed out that it was always seen in late December too, as that was when he had his sightings of the phantom.

Some folk came forward with 'identities' for the hooded spectre. Some said it was Walter de Lacy, who had fallen from the church tower back in the thirteenth century. Others suggested it may be the ghost of a monk who had allegedly been murdered at the altar. The organist's father claimed to have seen the monk inside the church, again in December.

After a while, the ghost story dissipated and the spectre was seen no more … until eight years later, when he made his appearance again. Several locals had claimed to see the figure around first light, when they were passing the church while on their way to work.

This spate of new ghost sightings brought pandemonium to the town when hundreds of would-be ghost hunters arrived at the churchyard in an effort to see the hooded phantom. On one occasion 200 people turned up in the hope of seeing the ghost. The authorities decided that enough was enough and so, in an effort to quell the unwanted attention, they declared that a joker had been caught in the act 'faking the ghost'– it worked. The crowds stopped their vigils and life returned to normal in the village. However, the ghost was not the result of a joker and more sightings occurred ... always in December.

To this day the ghost of St Peter's in Hereford is still said to be seen floating up the path and through the church doors, just like he always has. It seems to me that the ghost of St Peter's is nothing more that a residual ghost of a former monk or man of the cloth that has simply trodden this path many times when he was alive and continues to do so many years after he died. But why does he haunt so close to Christmas time? One can only wonder.

A Murdered Woman in White

On 20 December 1934 an electrician made his way to work; it was a day at work he would never forget. The *Lancashire Evening Post*, dated 2 January 1935, reported that the tradesman in question was heading to a property on New Hall Lane, in Preston, Lancashire. He was sent there by his boss to rewire the entire property before new tenants moved in. He got to work early in the morning and was there until the sun went down; it was a good, hard day's work.

Nearing the end of his shift, he entered one of the rooms on the first floor of the building when suddenly he felt 'strange'. An odd silence fell across the room which rattled him somewhat. Suddenly he felt that he was not alone. As he turned around to see if anyone was there with him, he was astonished to see a woman rise slowly out of the floor next to the door, who he described as rather tall, wearing a satin shroud and having black hair. What was most harrowing about her, however, was her large, piercing eyes. He dropped his tools and ran past her, down the stairs and out of the property. He never returned for his tools.

The owner of the property subsequently allowed four local men (including) a reporter from the *Lancashire Evening Post*) to spend the night at the 'haunted house' to see if they could see the ghost. Two of the others were 'psychic investigators' and the other was a medium. The medium claimed, upon entering the building, that she could see a woman with black hair. She said she was forty-two years old and went by the name of Margaret. Although the other investigators could not see the same woman as the medium, they *did* observe a rather strange white mist which had appeared in the corner of the room.

As it turned out, back in 1905 the building was owned by a butcher and his wife. The wife, it seems, had succumbed to the demon drink and had had a great stash of gin hidden away in a cupboard. The butcher became more upset at his wife's behaviour as each day she drank more and more. One day, much to his horror, he discovered that she was having an illicit affair with a local chap and was so angry that he promptly murdered her. It was this woman who locals believed had shown herself to the electrician.

THE EMLYN ARMS POLTERGEIST, SOUTH WALES

The Emlyn Arms Hotel is a wonderful little eighteenth-century inn located in the Carmarthenshire village of Llanarthney. It is a quiet little village pub where one can get good pub food and a fine pint of bitter in quiet and peaceful surroundings. However, back in 1909, during Christmas week, the inn was disturbed by a series of bewildering paranormal occurrences which have never been forgotten. The fact that it made many national and local newspapers also helped 'the haunting of the Emlyn Arms' to become a well known case.

The inn owner at the time, Mrs Meredith, had stayed behind while her husband went away for a week's holiday. It was during this week that the poltergeist struck. While tending to some of her cattle (which she kept at a nearby small property), she was mysteriously pelted by bricks and stones. The stones, which came from 'nowhere', bounced off the ground close to where she was walking and she was almost struck by them. Had they hit her, serious injury would surely have occurred. She put the stone-throwing down to 'up to no good' local youngsters and made her way back to the inn.

Later that evening, a young teenage servant girl was in her room when a thundering series of knocks were beaten upon her door. Thinking that someone was there, she ventured over to the door and opened it, but found that there was no one around. As she peered around the corner she was shocked to see that a candlestick that had been placed on a shelf along the corridor was hurtling towards her. She moved out of the way and the candlestick narrowly missed her head. Upon checking the area to see if anyone was there, she again found no one. This, by all accounts, was the start of the paranormal incidences within the walls of the Emlyn Arms.

A neighbour going by the name of Mrs Jenkins was walking past the property one night on her way home when she heard tremendously loud screaming coming from within. She and her niece, made their way over to the pub to see what was happening and, upon entering the inn, saw many household objects flying around of their own accord. She contacted her husband, who was the village policeman, and he arrived some time later to lend his assistance. He was a no-nonsense type of chap and so ventured forth straight into the now empty pub to apprehend the intruder responsible for the commotion. He admitted he could feel an 'eerie presence', but ventured into the house nonetheless.

A candlestick came hurtling towards her.

The village constable was called.

The policeman heard the sound of padding feet shuffling across the upper landing and so made his way upstairs to see who it was. Being sure he would catch the burglar in the act, he pounced round the corner – to find no one there. As he did so, he was attacked by an invisible assailant who threw glass bottles at him. The bottles smashed around him yet he could see no one actually throwing them.

Still convinced there was a burglar in the house, he made his way into the bedroom and looked under the bed. He found no one there. Suddenly, a vase came from nowhere and smashed right next to his head. By now half the village had gathered downstairs in the living area. They were all dumbstruck to see household objects being moved around and thrown about without any human assistance. It was a truly spectacular sight.

Mrs Meredith and the rest of the inn's residents had now decided that enough was enough and left the pub to stay with friends. The next day they all returned to the inn, whereupon the strange activity began once more. PC Jenkins, assisted by the villagers, formed a tight circle (like a cordon) around the inn to stop any intruder from escaping. However, no one was captured – for the simple reason that there was no one inside the inn causing the mayhem. PC Jenkins, and everyone else for that matter, was forced to conclude that the strange events at the Emlyn Arms were down to 'unexplained means'.

Not long after Christmas 1909, the disturbances that had plagued the pub for a week, ceased just as abruptly as it had begun.

four

CHRISTMAS INVESTIGATIONS

The following chapter contains previously unpublished investigation reports from the personal files of the author Darren W. Ritson.

A NOT SO SILENT NIGHT: DOXFORD HOUSE
CHRISTMAS INVESTIGATIONS 2008 – PART ONE

Doxford House is a magnificent privately owned stately home in the Silksworth area of Sunderland and on Saturday, 1 December 2008 it belonged to GHOST (Ghost and Hauntings Overnight Surveillance Team). Situated on land known as 'Silksworth manorial lands', which was once owned by a family named Robinson, Doxford House is a spectacular eighteenth-century mansion built by William Johnson between 1775 and 1780. It is said that the land it was built on was separated from Silksworth manorial lands' main estate sometime before the 1600s and, more interestingly, a medieval chapel is said to lie under the ground at the side of this beautiful mansion.

A Mr H. Hopper of Durham acquired the house after William Johnson's death in 1792; he was the family lawyer and a good friend of William Johnson. Mr Hopper subsequently left it to his

Doxford House in Sunderland.

nephew, Thomas Hopper. His daughter, Pricilla Marie Hopper, married General Charles Beckwith and moved into the house. It was at this time that the front entrance to the house was constructed and adorned with the Beckwith coat of arms. It is a magnificent piece of stonemasonry that can still be seen to this day. In 1890, the Beckwith family moved to Shropshire and the estate was leased to a man named John Craven. When he died in 1902, a lease was taken up for the house by a man called Charles Doxford, who laid out the gardens and the lake before the First World War. He was a wealthy shipbuilder at that time and certainly had the money, and time, to do this. It was his daughter, Aline Doxford, who lived at the house after Charles's death in 1935.

The house is believed to be haunted by the ghost of General Beckwith, with his shade being seen on the grand staircase and in the large bedroom upstairs many times since the 1930s. This sighting usually occurs around Christmas time, or at least in the month of December, so we were in the house at the right time of year to maybe catch of glimpse of this elusive figure. It is also believed that the ghost of Aline Doxford may still reside in the property too. There is an unsubstantiated claim that Aline may

The main entrance / foyer area of Doxford House. (Courtesy of Drew Bartley)

have held lurid sexual gatherings with her many friends, who, incidentally, were all said to be women. It is also reputed that a certain room on the ground floor situated in the semi-circular side wing, is the room where Aline Doxford once locked herself in for weeks at a time to carry out Ouija board sessions. Whatever went on there in the past had certainly left its mark on the building.

The property owner, Phil Jeffries, told GHOST that his two Alsatian dogs will simply not venture upstairs in the house. They say dogs have a 'sixth sense' and can see and sense things that humans can't. If this is the case, it would seem that there is something lurking on the upper floors which keeps these fierce guard dogs at bay.

We arrived at the building on 1 December 2008 at 1.30 p.m. so that we could have a look around the house during the daylight hours. We were met by the property owner, and the GHOST team – Yvonne Moore, Ralph Keeton, Drew Bartley, Fiona Vipond and myself – ventured inside this magnificent stately home for the first time. We walked into a long corridor that seemed to go on forever. The atmosphere began to take a hold and as we walked along, passing over fifty small rooms along the way, we could sense that this old building really did have secrets hidden deep within. As we approached the end of the long corridor a magnificent foyer and seventeenth-century wooden staircase greeted us. Under the stairwell, directly ahead of where we stood, was a beautiful alcove with seats either side of an old and striking fireplace. Opposite this was the semi-circular wing and Aline's 'Ouija room'.

It was in this room where, many years ago, workmen carrying out construction on the building had their tea breaks. One workman, said to be a big burly chap and not afraid of anything, sat down to his morning cuppa and breakfast sandwich. After enjoying his break he attempted to stand up but found he could not. Something had grabbed hold of his shoulders and pressed downwards on him, pinning him down and stopping him from getting up to his feet. These feelings went on for a minute or so before they subsided. Said to be 'terrified' and 'chilled to the bone', the workman fled the premises and never returned.

Doxford House contains many huge rooms with high and original Italian-style Renaissance ceilings and grand fireplaces.

To our right were the main entrance and a marvellous Victorian-style conservatory, which was festooned with exotic plants and decked out with garden ornaments and old furniture. A large stone water feature with granite stairs going up and around it from either side, led us to the nineteenth-century addition to the house, which was the entrance folly that bares the Doxford coat of arms.

After a great deal of time exploring the premises, we ventured outside into the gardens. Winter blizzards had brought a blanket of snow, which gave the gardens something of a magical Yuletide feel. The gardens are just as impressive as the house, with a giant oak tree dominating the grounds, casting a dark and foreboding shadow over the great house.

The afternoon at Doxford House was a worthwhile exercise; not only did it give us time to get to know the building and its

The main stairwell, where General Beckwith's ghost has been seen on countless occasions. (Courtesy of Drew Bartley)

layout, but one or two strange occurrences were also reported. Having a medium with us, we expected a few readings and Ralph Keeton certainly provided us with some interesting facts. Ralph is a good friend of our team and was invited along by GHOST to assist in our investigations. He told us that he picked up on 'lesbian parties and orgies' along with a feeling of 'witchcraft and occultism'. This was his first hit of the day because, if the reader recalls, it was alleged that this went on in the house in days gone by. Ralph couldn't possibly have researched this as the source of information came from those that knew Miss Aline Doxford personally.

Also picked up by Ralph was the spirit of a little girl, who was somehow left out on a balcony or a landing area. The Ouija board room was identified by Ralph, even though he was unaware of Ouija board sessions being held there, and he also identified two other spirits in Doxford House. One of those was on the main stairwell, where he saw a black mass come swirling up from the ground floor, straight past him and up to the top of the building. It happened in a split second, but the most significant thing about this sighting was that Yvonne Moore saw it too.

Fiona also experienced something anomalous during the course of the afternoon. While walking along the long corridor that leads to the bottom of the staircase, she noticed behind one of the many doors, which happened to be open an inch or so, a shadow that seemed to block out the light. Upon stopping to take a closer look, the shadow moved away from the gap in the door, thus letting back in the light from outside. It was as if someone was standing behind the door casting its shadow up the wall and blocking out the light. She burst in through the door but found no one there.

Drew also experienced an odd happening: twice he saw what looked like a black shape move quickly across the floor. He only saw it out of the corner of his eye, and at first he thought it was a cat scurrying across the floor. However, he saw it again while standing on the first floor on the stairs. I think I was the only one that afternoon that didn't experience anything. Still, we had yet to return for the investigation.

Before the investigation began, I asked Ralph to make his predictions to see if he could tell us what would happen during the investigations. He said:

> I think it's going to be very exciting, I think we are going to see something … definitely. I definitely want to talk about a door closing or opening on its own … certainly in one of the rooms I know we are going to hear a voice, we are going to hear somebody, we are going to get auditory, we are going to get visual communication without a doubt.

Rather clear-cut prophesies and, amazingly, as you will shortly hear, accurate too. We all arrived back at Doxford House at 10 p.m. The place was shrouded in darkness (there was no electricity supply) and the atmosphere felt entirely different to our afternoon investigation.

GHOST were joined by a number of guests, mostly members of the family who own Doxford House, but it was anticipated they would only stay for an hour or so before becoming extremely bored, and cold. We were correct, as most of the guests vacated the premises just after midnight, leaving the team to plod on until sunrise. Trigger objects and motion sensors were placed around the older part of Doxford House, including a crucifix on the main stairwell, and motion sensors on the stairs, in the Ouija room, and in doorways to certain rooms. A night-vision video recorder was also left running all night and was trained on the stairwell. If General Beckwith appeared in his usual location, we should catch him on tape.

At 10.22 p.m. we were preparing to begin the investigation when suddenly the tape from inside Drew's video camera ejected itself. Drew claims to have been holding the camera with its correct handle and states 'there should be no reason for the eject mechanism to have been triggered'. At 10.45 p.m. we began the vigil at the foot of the stairwell with Drew, Andrew Hughes, Lloyd, and myself. We called out to the atmosphere to see if we could get any responses from the netherworld, but to no avail and, after sitting quietly at the foot of the stairwell for a time, nothing occurred. We then moved into the 'Ouija room', closed the door and began to call out again. Once more we had no response whatsoever. At midnight we all heard the sound of a footfall followed by a single bang. No one was moving at the time and we called out once more to see if we could get more 'signs'.

We then headed into another of the large rooms on the lower floor, where we sat in silence for a while. Nothing major occurred in this room, however there were two minor incidents. A rustling of paper was heard by Lloyd and myself coming from a corner of the room where there was about 250 old books, literally strewn all over the place. Lloyd said the noise we heard resembled the rustling you would get if you unwrapped a boiled sweet. Whatever it was, it was strange to say the least. Even stranger was the fact that I had asked the spirits to try and make their presence known to us by rustling one of the book pages. The other thing that occurred was that the temperature of the room dropped noticeably and, at the same time, a dull thud was heard coming from somewhere within the darkness. At 11.20 p.m. we retired to the base room for a short break.

I asked Fiona if anything had occurred during her first vigil, which was on the top-floor area and in the loft. She told me that guest investigator Gemma Carrick had had a bit of an experience:

> We were up in the loft and I was stood where Fiona had been standing previously, I suddenly felt a draught on my leg. Fiona had been standing in this spot and had also felt a draught and that is why we swapped places, to see if I could also feel it. As I could feel the draught the room temperature dropped from a fluctuation between 14–17 degrees Celsius to 1 degree.

That was a staggering temperature drop of at least 13 degrees Celsius, which is quite phenomenal to say the least. Fiona said the room was foreboding and stated that 'someone didn't want us there'. Another interesting odd occurrence took place when Yvonne's son, Malcolm Moore, saw a movement from behind one of the wooden beams. Described as 'something darting behind the beam', this anomaly was also caught on Fiona's night-vision video camera. As the camera pans to the right, you can clearly see something zip across the screen from the left and go behind the wooden beam. On studying the footage in super slow motion you can see the anomaly (which is likened to a head) move behind the beam. As the main anomaly disappears, it is followed by wisps of … well, we have no idea what they are.

Ralph's group reported some odd activity too. He was on the middle floor with his group and told me that they had heard a tremendous thud on the floor while they were calling out, asking for phenomena. It was as though someone had a broom handle and thumped the ceiling from downstairs (only my group was in the room below and we heard nothing). Ralph then asked for more phenomena and the whole group heard what they thought was our group chatting to ourselves. Our group, during our vigil, did indeed communicate with one another but we whispered when doing so. There was no way the voices that Ralph and his group heard were ours, so whose voices were they? It remains a mystery.

After our break it was time for the second vigil. Some of the guests had left the premises, which left the rest of those present to re-group to continue with the investigation. My new group consisted of Ralph, Gemma, Lloyd and Mark Winter and we were investigating the top floor. We began our vigil at the very top of the old stairwell and, almost straight away, Ralph began to tell us what he was picking up. Ralph began pacing back and forth and up and down the stairs and was adamant he was picking up on a spirit. Suddenly he called out, 'Who is there, who is there? There is someone on the stairs.' At that point I clearly saw someone, or something, move down the stairs and with some considerable speed. It moved swiftly and silently as it flitted from one section of the stairs to another, lit up by the distant light of street lamps coming in through the windows. It then disappeared into the darkness.

Lloyd confirms that he also saw the movement under the stairs we were standing on, so that brings the total number of witnesses to the sighting to three. At 12.15 a.m. we all heard a noise that sounded like a cross between a growl and a hum coming from somewhere on the stairwell. What it was we have no idea. It was now 12.17 a.m. and we decided to venture into the loft space. One by one we clambered up the steep wooden steps and into the loft. While in there, we all experienced a number of cold rushes of air, but after looking around for a cause we found an aperture in the ceiling from which the cold breezes probably came.

A thump, thump, thump noise was then heard by myself and Ralph, for which no explanation could be found. Then the sound of a guttural breath was heard by all present and everyone said that it was definitely not them that produced it. Ralph then heard another growling type noise coming from within the loft space but said it was a psychic sound – in other words because Ralph was the medium he was the only one to hear it. After a while, it seemed to quieten down a little so we made our way back down to the top floor.

We then went to investigate the newer wing of Doxford House and Ralph found himself being pulled on the arm as we walked past room 21. Earlier on during a walk around Gemma had lost her breath and found her chest to be getting 'quite tight' outside room 21. A guest investigator also reported that she felt unwell and said her legs 'tingled' while standing outside this particular room. Gemma thought nothing of it until Ralph mentioned that he felt something tug on his arm. We thought room 21 could be trying to tell us something so we all went inside. As it happened, room 21 provided us with amazing auditory phenomena in the form of a female voice. It must be stressed that we were all standing in silence and everyone there, all five of us, heard this voice. It simply said, 'I am coming in.'

At first we thought it was a voice coming through on the walkie-talkie, but the walkie-talkie was actually turned off at the time. This occurred at 12.55 a.m. and it dumbfounded us all. After discussing the voice (which unfortunately was not picked up on video or dictation machine) we made our way back to the top of the stairs. It was here we all experienced the most perplexing phenomena of the entire night. Looking along the corridor, Ralph spotted the spirit form of a child that seemed to be moving back and forth in the corridor. I, at this point, was down the stairs and looking out of the window. Suddenly, Lloyd said in a surprised voice, 'Bloody hell, I can see her!'

When Lloyd announced that he too could see what Ralph was looking at, I realised that it wasn't just Ralph psychically seeing things. I bolted up the stairs and looked along the corridor and, to my utter astonishment, I too saw what looked liked a white figure moving around. It flittered hither and thither and it looked as though it was a young girl dancing around. We watched this in total disbelief for about five minutes or so until another, taller figure of a woman materialised next to the smaller one. They both then disappeared into the darkness of the corridor, not to be seen again. It was as though the older lady had come for the young girl.

Four people in the group witnessed this spectacle. Mark was filming it on his video recorder but could see nothing. When he took his eyes from the camera to look down the corridor (as his viewfinder was closed), his vision was distorted. This was due to the fact that he was looking into darkness after looking into the light. The video camera failed to pick up this amazing phenomenon, but that is not surprising. It was, however, very disappointing. How many times do you hear of investigators hearing voices that have been recorded on tape or EVP machines but do not hear anything at the time of recording? Likewise you can hear footsteps, murmurs, bangs and raps with your ears, and not pick them up on tape. Sometimes, for example, a group of six people may be present when a ghost shows itself and although they are all looking in the same direction, only two people see it. The same principal, I feel, could apply to this sighting as four witnesses watched it yet the camera failed to pick it up.

Could it have been our eyes playing tricks on us in the dark? Maybe so, but all four of us? Could it have been a group hallucination? Maybe it was caused by the power of suggestion after Ralph mentioned what he could see. Once the thought had been implanted into our heads, maybe we were all led to Ralph's pacing? (Pacing and leading is a technique used by hypnotists to build a rapport with the subject. He can set the pace for example, in his breathing or perhaps in his state of relaxation, and then lead his subject into a close bond in order to induce the trance-like state, therefore disabling his subconscious mind far quicker and easier than normal and giving him the influence to take away any reservations or inhibitions the subject may have.)

I am not saying Ralph did this on purpose to fool everyone into thinking that they were seeing ghosts; on the contrary, it may have occurred on a subconscious level, without him even knowing he was doing it. This happens all the time in everyday life. For example, if you yawn in a room full of people, and then sniff, the chances are that others in the room will soon yawn and then sniff. This is pacing and leading on a subconscious level and it could have happened when we all saw the figures. Having said that, it is also perfectly possibly that we could all have seen a genuine apparition.

Drew reported that during his vigil Andrew Local (one of our guests) thought he saw a figure standing in the doorway in the entrance foyer at the bottom of the stairs. He walked over with his EMF meter and ventured a little way down the corridor. Suddenly, the EMF meter spiked, giving Drew a sharp reading of around 4mg (Milligaus). He decided to step back and ask the spirit (if indeed there was one there) to come closer, but nothing happened. He then ventured forwards, EMF meter held flat on his hand, and, sure enough, it spiked again. Apart from these instances, nothing much else was reported as most taps and bumps that were heard had rational explanations found for them.

Our next vigil saw my group investigating the 'Ouija board' room and, upon entering the room, I closed the door behind me, properly. I say properly because it must be noted that, as I turned and walked into the room to check on the trigger object, the door silently swung back open. As I turned around to say something to the group, I saw Ralph walking towards the open door with his arm outstretched, saying, 'I am just going to shut the door' and I realised that, no sooner had I closed the door tightly in its frame, it had opened back up behind me. Lloyd can confirm that I did indeed close the door, however, no one saw it re-open. It was a very eerie experience.

A picture of the door from inside Aline Doxford's 'ouija board room'. This door has been seen to open on its own on at least three occasions, twice by the author and Ralph Keeton, and once by Drew Bartley. The door was securely closed on each of these occasions and no explanation was ever found for it.

Later on, we all clearly heard a voice that sounded like Drew calling my name 'Darren' from the main foyer. We ventured out into the main entrance area to find no one there at all. I subsequently called out to Drew to ask him if it was indeed he who had said my name and got no reply. I called him again and this time I heard him answer, but he was far off in the distance. It was clear to us that it was not Drew that called out my name as he was far away at that time in his respective location, so who called out my name? There was no one else around.

This is the second time on my paranormal investigations that my name had been called out by an alleged spirit person. The first time it occurred was on an investigation in July 2006 and it was caught on tape. This time it was heard by all the investigators in my group but not recorded.

The conservatory area of Doxford House. (Courtesy of Drew Bartley)

We called out to the atmosphere, tried a séance followed by a table-tipping experiment in the hope that we got more odd activity, but the rest of this vigil proved fruitless. We then moved into the main entrance area and joined up with other groups to try a séance. A number of things occurred which we found most peculiar, including the motion sensors that were situated on the stairwell being activated when Ralph was calling out. A sigh was heard along with some laughter, and some odd sparkly silvery specks of light seemed to float down the stairwell. What they were is anyone's guess but most of the group there saw them. Along with the temperature dropping, this séance proved rather interesting.

After another break we all ventured back onto the stairwell for one final vigil. We sat out on the stairwell for about forty-five minutes calling out and generally observing. Ralph and Andrew local claimed to hear a scream but no one else did. Others felt temperature changes and cold spots throughout the vigil. It must be noted that it was now about 3 a.m. on an icy morning in December and everyone was naturally cold and tired. The investigation had proved to be really good, with some rather bizarre things occurring. Ralph's prediction prior to the investigation regarding what we would experience turned out correct with the door opening, a voice being heard, auditory phenomena (including the voice), seeing something, and more besides. 'I think it's going to be very exciting,' he had said, and how right he was.

Doxford House near Christmas time was always going to be an exciting venture and we are confident that it will no doubt reveal all its hidden secrets and ghosts to our research team over the coming years. Our next investigation was held a week or so after Christmas Day in early January 2009. The story of our not so 'silent night' follows.

A NOT SO 'SILENT NIGHT': DOXFORD HOUSE CHRISTMAS INVESTIGATIONS 2009 – PART TWO

It had been a few weeks or so since our first investigation at the magnificent Doxford House, and, for a house that had never been investigated prior to the Ghosts and Hauntings Overnight Surveillance Team going in, it certainly seemed to prove its worth. Drew and Fiona had visited Doxford House on a number of other occasions since the first investigation before Christmas 2008, not as investigators, but as cleaners. The house, although in rather good condition considering its circumstances, was rather messy, with reminders of the time when it was once home to a thousand students. They say the more time you spend in 'haunted houses' the more chance you have of witnessing paranormal activity, and cleaning the house up and getting it into a safe condition for investigators would have been an ideal opportunity to do this.

I asked Drew and Fiona if they happened to encounter any paranormal or odd happenings during the few occasions they visited the house to clean it up, but nothing of an unusual nature had occurred during Drew and Fiona's clean-up process. However, a good friend of Fiona's, a lady called Pat (who also happens to own a very well known haunted establishment), was a woman who had worked at Doxford House as a caretaker/manager/ cleaner. We were told that during the many years that she worked there, she experienced what she considered to be 'hundreds of odd happenings' and 'saw all sorts of things'. Whether these experiences are subjective or objective we will never know, as the woman in question sadly died in August 2008. Being denied the chance to interview someone who could have been a 'prized witness' is of course a blow for the team as every piece of witness testimony, even the somewhat trivial data, can be of the utmost importance to us. Nevertheless, it is simply interesting to note that yet another of the frequenters of Doxford House reported strange things occurring and although we can't document what it was she experienced, we can record the fact that she thought the house was haunted.

Early in January 2009 we commenced with our second investigation. Drew, Fiona, Ralph Keeton, Nikki Austwicke, Trevor Walker and Yvonne Moore visited the house on the afternoon of the investigation to make sure all was well for the evening to come. That evening, Drew told the rest of the GHOST team what had occurred:

> This afternoon we had a little tour around and, just before leaving, we were on the second-floor stairwell, ready to come down, when I heard a door slamming somewhere upstairs near the top landing, and it was quite loud too. I then asked if everyone else heard the door closing and they all replied yes. Ralph then called out, and asked whomever

it was to do the same thing again and the door bloody well slammed again. Then, to our astonishment, we all heard the sound of footsteps walking along the top corridor; no one else was in the building and we were all accounted for. I must also add that this afternoon the sun was shining and it was a nice calm day, it was nothing like the windy conditions that we are experiencing tonight.

Interestingly, it was here, on this top corridor, that I had a nerve-racking experience, an experience that I had never encountered before in all my years of frequenting haunted locales, and which literally chilled me to the bone – but more of that later.

The investigation started and hopes were high of getting something good documented. Along with myself, Drew, Fiona and Mark, and the usual guests Ryan Bartley, Jim and Paul Collins, ex-team member Paul Dixon joined us, as did Ralph Keeton, Nikki Austwicke and their guest Trevor Walker. The weather was very cold and, it must be stressed on this particular night the wind was howling to such a degree we all thought the house would be blown down. Due to the fact there were a few broken windows that still need repairing in the house, any draughts, temperature drops, or any other phenomena for that matter, had to be seriously considered before a decision on whether or not it may have had paranormal origin.

It was 10.30 p.m. and we got on with the pre-investigation responsibilities with our baseline tests being carried out, followed by the setting up of the lock-off video cameras, the trigger experiments and the placing of the motion sensors and beam barriers. The baselines proved rather straightforward due to the winds outside. The squeaky floorboards were traced throughout the house, and the EMF surveys provided the investigators with no readings whatsoever. We placed beam barriers on each flight of the grand stairwell, set a video camera recording on the lower section of the stairwell – in the hope of recording the infamous spectre of General Beckwith, and a number of trigger objects were placed around the premises. A cross was placed on the floor in the master bedroom (we used this as a base room on our first investigation and, for whatever reason, it was not investigated, even though there are accounts of the General's ghost being seen in this room), and a beautiful ornamental Ouija board was placed on the table in what we have now coined the 'Ouija board room'. Finally, a child's cuddly toy was placed on the fire extinguisher stand mounted to the wall in the passageway on the upper level of the house.

Prior to recording what happened on our night's vigil, I will relate to you some odd activity that was reported by Ralph Keeton while the tour of the house was being carried out for those individuals who had not been there before. He told me that during the walk around he picked up on the name 'Monica'. After saying the name out loud, the voice of a young girl was said to have been heard. A few knocks and taps were heard too that were thought to have had paranormal origin. Other odd activity was recorded by others, and not in the main house area.

During a break before the main event, we were downstairs at the back door near the car park in what was a newer section of the building. At 11 p.m. Drew noticed that the door to the disabled toilet and shower room was wide open and he was pretty sure that it had just been closed. He asked everyone if they had used the toilet in there and perhaps left the door open, to which they all replied 'no'. Besides, there is another toilet just a few yards away that everyone preferred to use. In fact, I had just used it, and, upon coming out, I walked past the disabled toilet and shower room and remember distinctly that the door was indeed closed.

Drew and I stood in the corridor to discuss this most recent occurrence and during our talk we were disturbed by what sounded like a harrowing wail coming from along the long dark corridor. Whatever it was, it seemed to eminate from the original part of Doxford House, but we knew the house was empty. Although I am positive that it sounded nothing like wind there is still a possibility that it could have been. However, for the rest of the night no other sounds were heard similar to the 'wail', even though the wind continued to blow until the early hours.

Now it was time to head off into the cold, dark night and begin our second attempt at contacting the ghosts of Doxford House. We split up into our teams and headed off to our respective vigil locations. My group, which consisted of Ralph, Nikki, Trevor, Paul and myself, investigated the 'Ouija board room' on the bottom floor, while Fiona's group, which consisted of Yvonne, Mark Winter and of course Fiona, staked out the middle floor. Drew's group, consisting of Ryan, Paul Dixon and Jim, investigated the top level of the building. It was 11.20 p.m.

Upon entering the 'Ouija board room' I asked Ralph and Trevor if they were picking anything up on a spiritual level, to which they replied 'not at the minute'. No sooner had we walked into the room and closed the door it sprang open. This, of course, happened in our first investigation and, oddly enough, it was when my group was investigating the room, and it was also in the presence of Ralph Keeton. It was I who closed the door tightly on the first investigation but this time it was Ralph, who also claimed to have shut it properly. Although it was windy outside we don't think that enough wind or resulting draughts could have been responsible for the opening of this door simply because a) the door was closed tight, and b) this door was nowhere near any broken windows, besides, all other doors in the vicinity were also tightly closed, isolating this door. If the draught had came in from inside the Ouija board room it could hardly have pulled the door open, as it would have been blowing against the way the door opens, anyway, no windows were broken and no draughts were reported in this particular room. If, however, it was by some chance the wind, then this still doesn't explain how the door opened of its own volition on our first investigation on 1 December 2008, when no wind at all was blowing outside. Both Ralph and I feel that this door could be one to watch in future investigations, as there seems to be a pattern emerging with it.

Lots of famous haunted buildings have certain areas and certain reported phenomena associated within those areas, such as a door at Washington Old Hall in Tyne and Wear. It is said that the door to the Panelled Room is always found open after it has been closed, and visa-versa. One wonders if the former residents of Doxford House, or even perhaps those that have worked there, experienced this particular door opening on its own.

The only other odd occurrences (apart from knocks and taps that could have been explained away naturally due to the wind, and other experiences which were largely subjective) was hearing a sigh or a breath coming from the door area. Ralph, Nikki and Trevor all heard this. But the most interesting phenomena documented in this vigil were the sound of heavy thumps coming from the master bedroom upstairs – where the General had often been seen – and which sounded incredibly like heavy footfalls. In fact, the thumps were so heavy that the light fittings on the ceiling in our room rattled and clinked violently. After hearing these thumps, I located and then spoke to the team that was investigating this level in order to determine where exactly they were at the time the thumps were heard. As I was talking to Fiona, Yvonne and Mark (while they were actually standing on the stairs and in my view), Paul Collins and Ralph continued to hear the heavy thumping and rattling around the ceiling area which came from the room above. This verified to all in my group that there was no one in that room at the time of the thumps being heard on the second occasion. Therefore we can safely presume the first set of thumps were anomalous too.

Fiona's group experienced a little odd phenomenon too. They first ventured into the newer section of the building, where they proceeded to call out to the atmosphere in the hope of making contact with someone, but to no avail. Mark claims to have seen something through a glass window (but what it was he could not say), so they ventured into the area where it was seen, and continued to call out. The door next to where they were standing was then said to have rattled and banged upon their command,

The light fittings rattled due to heavy footfalls in the room above. Investigations showed that no one was in the above room at the time of the ghostly footfalls.

although the investigators did suspect it could have been the wind, since there was a broken window in this particular room. At the end of their vigil they all heard a sigh or breath which, oddly, seemed to have occurred at the same time as Ralph, Nikki and Trevor heard a sigh while in the Ouija room. Drew's group experienced nothing that could be classed as remotely paranormal, as all knocks, bumps and draughts were sensibly ruled out.

On our way to our break, I decided to leave my EVP machine recording in the main foyer area and subsequently left it on the mantelpiece situated under the grand stairwell. The recording lasted for thirty minutes and there was nothing on it. On our way to our second location I picked up the EVP recorder and continued to my next location, which was the top floor. Drew's team investigated the middle floor while Fiona's stayed on the bottom level of the house.

I mentioned earlier that I had had a nerve-racking experience that chilled me to the bone, and it was in this vigil location that it occurred. We got settled in to the investigation and began to call out. I took some digital stills and made some EVP recordings, but to no avail, so I joined the rest of the group that were standing along the passageway. Suddenly, after Ralph had called out, we all heard two thumps or bangs. They seemed to come from the top of the stairwell area, but upon examining the area we found nothing out of place. It was duly noted that the wind seemed to have calmed down considerably at this time as we could not hear it from inside the premises, nor could we see the large tree that stands at the front of the house swaying all was calm. After asking for the banging to recommence, we all heard it again and it was most fascinating to say the least.

The shock came thirty minutes into the vigil when I decided to venture forth down the passageway with EVP machine in hand after a male grunt was heard coming from that area. As I was preparing my EVP machine for this experiment, everyone present except me then heard a male voice cry 'Ouch' as if someone was being hurt. I duly noted down these incidences and headed off to make my recordings.

I had taken only three or four steps and was parallel with the door to room 1, which stood across from room 29. Suddenly, from nowhere, came a feeling that someone was running a hand across my face. At the same time I heard a noise that I can only describe as a 'sizzling static' followed by two distinct footfalls right in front of me. I thought to myself 'something is coming toward me' and before I even had a chance to register this thought, I was overcome with an ice-cold sensation inside my body, accompanied by a feeling of absolute terror. This feeling lasted for only a brief second or so before it dissipated, leaving me shocked, shaken and surprised. As crazy as it sounds, I think that something, I don't know what, went through me!

On my tape I said just after the incident, 'I have never felt anything like that, ever, on an investigation – I honestly think that something has just walked through me, and that is bloody frightening.'

After five minutes or so after the incident, and while discussing it with the group, I felt something touch the top of my head. At this point in the investigation however, I was jumping at shadows and everything else come to think about it. At one point I even got a fright when I leaned against the wall, simply because the wall was cold. I was absolutely useless to myself and the group, due to the terrifying experience, so, for the obvious reasons, I took it upon myself to end this vigil. Upon leaving the area I again left my EVP machine recording and this time it recorded for nearly one hour. On it was various knocks, taps and noises that I concluded were not of a paranormal nature.

Fiona's group yielded no results; although one or two things did occur, rational explanations were found for them. Drew and his group yet again experienced nothing at all. However, in between these vigils it was noted by an investigator that the Ouija board that had been left as a trigger object had been moved. At first it looked as though the actual planchette had been moved because it was not central (the way it had been left) but, after looking closer at it, we realised that the round glass plate that is used to cover and protect the actual Ouija board was what had been moved, with the planchette still being central to that. Regardless, we had had a result in regards to trigger objects. It may be no coincidence too that the trigger object of the Ouija board actually moved in the very room where Lady Doxford conducted her Ouija board sessions.

The ouija board that was used as a trigger object during our investigations. The protective glass sheet that covers the board was found to have been 'shifted' from its position. No one was in the actual room at the time.

At 2 a.m. we all gathered in the Ouija board room in an attempt to contact Lady Doxford via her own favourite form of spirit contact – the board! To cut a long story short, the whole session lasted about ninety minutes with eighty of those minutes being a complete waste of time. In the last ten minutes the planchette did actually move around the table with the letter 'W' being established, but, as per normal with Ouija sessions, the messages came jumbled up and were pure gibberish.

The last vigil of the night was spent investigating the foyer area of the house, as this had been one of the most interesting areas that had not yet been fully investigated. As it happened, we recorded nothing anomalous whatsoever, although Ralph did pick up on a young girl. He is adamant that a young girl haunts this house, but who she is and whether we can find her historical records remains to be seen. I attempted a number of five-minute EVP experiments, asking certain questions and leaving enough space between the questions for any alleged spirits or ghosts to answer. After three or four attempts and recording nothing we gave up. It was now about 4.30 a.m. and everyone was becoming really tired. The other groups all met up in the base room, but they had nothing further to report; any apparent phenomena witnessed was put down to sheer tiredness. It is known on investigations for the investigators to become so tired they begin to encounter auditory, and quite often visual, hallucinations; not good for an objective investigation. Due to this factor, we all decided that now was the time to wrap it up.

All in all, this second investigation proved to be great for some, and not so great for others, but that's the way ghost hunting goes. The thumps and bumps that were heard in the Ouija room (from upstairs) during our vigil there were quite impressive, especially as they made the lights rattle in the room below. The fact the Ouija room door opened for the second time while Ralph and I were there to see it again is rather interesting too. In regards to what happened to me on the upper level of the building, well … who can say for sure. In retrospect it really does give me the

Doxford House from the rear. (Courtesy of Drew Bartley)

chills thinking about what happened, but was it really a spirit that walked through me? Or was it something else, something psychological? Maybe only time will tell. Further investigations inside this rambling old building in Sunderland have subsequently been carried out. Results of these investigations will hopefully be published soon.

The fact remains that the first two investigations to be held at Doxford House yielded some really extraordinary results to say the least and one can not help but wonder, was it really due to being so close to the festive season? One just before and one just after Yuletide. Who can say? I will leave that for you to decide.

CHRISTMAS INVESTIGATION 2009: SHOP 44, AND SHOP 22, THE SHAMBLES IN YORK

On the night of 4 December 2009 GHOST arrived in the city of York to conduct a double Christmas investigation at numbers 22 and 44 The Shambles. We arrived at the top of the famous Shambles at 9 p.m. and were met by shop owner, Simon Cox, who took us down to his wonderful gift shops. As we entered the first shop, we were shown to the café section of the premises at the rear; this was to be used as our base room.

The building of number 44 is around 400 years old and has three floors. On each floor there is a passage leading to two rooms, one at the front and one overlooking the market square at the rear. The rooms on the upper level are used as storage, while the downstairs rooms are used for the gift shop and small café. The building also houses an ancient wooden stairwell, which links all these old rooms and landings together.

Number 22 The Shambles is entirely different. It is a much smaller shop by far, but this property has a hidden gem, well, two to be precise. Under the floor in the shop were two trapdoors. Trapdoor one led down into an old, foreboding cellar and tall stepladders were needed to get down into it. It is a large roomy area and, by all accounts, well worth investigating. Trapdoor two was the *pièce de résistance*. After negotiating your way down some old stone steps, you are led into another cellar area. This cellar leads you under the cobbled road that is The Shambles and under the neighbouring church which stands at the foot of The Shambles.

We unpacked our equipment and prepared for the investigation to come. Before we set about conducting the usual baseline tests prior to our investigation, I needed to speak to the individuals who worked in the shop. Of course, team member Fiona Vipond had already gleaned some information regarding the ghosts from Simon on her pre-investigation visit, and it was – it must be said – thanks to Fiona that we were here in the first place; but, for

York Minster, one of the most notable features of this haunted city and not far from the haunted Shambles.

Number 44 The Shambles. This haunted giftshop and café was the scene of our Christmas investigation in 2009. (Courtesy of Mark Winter)

my notes and for my personal files, I needed to interview those people who had had first-hand experiences with the alleged denizens.

I first spoke to Simon Cox and he informed me that his sister-in-law, Chantelle, had heard something rather strange while alone in the shop. Simon went on to tell me that his wife had seen a ghost of a woman dressed in black on the stairs of the property. I asked him if he knew who any of these ethereal visitors could be and he replied that he did not. This ghost was seen only eight weeks prior to our visit, so it seemed that the activity occurring within these premises were ongoing.

I then asked Simon if anything had occurred since Fiona's first visit to the shop. He told me that a number of things had indeed taken place. He said that he had heard a growling noise on three occasions when no one was around, and mentioned that, for no reason, 'strange stenches' come from nowhere and then, as suddenly as they appeared, disappeared. As recently as the night before our investigation (on 3 December 2009) a door had opened for no apparent reason. In total, six different individuals claimed to have experienced paranormal phenomena at the premises and the staff and Simon were convinced it was haunted.

In regards to the ghostly activity in his other shop, number 22, he told me that objects fly off the stands and shelves (key rings, novelty signs etc.). He also said that the stands have been seen to spin around, which of course sends all the merchandise flying off, and bells have been heard ringing inside the shop. I asked what type of bells they were, as his shop is only yards away from the church. He laughed and explained they were little hand bells, the sort that people use on their reception desks when people need to 'ring for attention'.

'Not church bells then,' I said.

'No,' he replied.

After speaking to Simon, I spoke to his sister-in-law, Chantelle Morris. Chantelle works in the shop at number 44 as an assistant in the café area. After asking her if she had had any experiences or 'brushes with the paranormal' while working in the property, she informed me that she had. I asked her what she had experienced and she replied that she had heard a 'growling' noise when she was standing at the bottom of the stairs. She said it was clear and definite, and, on looking around for people, to see if they were playing jokes, she found no one; it appeared that she was in the building on her own. On another occasion, Chantelle's sister reported that she had seen a 'weird' man walk along the passageway and enter the café area of the building. When the two women both ventured in, to see who it was, the room was empty, but the door to the storage room (which leads nowhere) was wide open! No one was found.

Chantelle then went on to tell me about a visitor who came to the shop (about six months prior to our visit, making it around May 2009) who had supposedly seen an apparition of a man who 'looked like a headteacher' standing in the corner of the room. This man had a young boy sitting on his shoulders and both were dressed in old-style attire. Then, within a blink of an eye, they were gone. York is, of course, famous for its ghostly inhabitants and it is said that within the walls of this ancient city there are 140 of them. Well, we can say now that there are potentially at least another six.

Ralph Keeton, the team medium, arrived in York at about 7 p.m. and made his way to the shop. By the time I arrived he had picked up on a number of things of interest. I had a quick chat with him in a quiet room on the second floor prior to the investigation and this is what he said:

> When I first came in and explained what I do, my role on the team, I was met by this spirit woman. When I saw this woman, I had the feeling she was blind in one eye. It was as though I felt a cloudy sensation across the left-hand side of my face and eye, and it was this that led me to believe she was blind. A stroke came to mind too. Perhaps she had had a stroke. Of course, when I mentioned this I was astonished to find out the ghost of a woman has been seen on the

An atmospheric view of The Shambles, York's oldest cobbled street. (Julie Olley)

A view of York's oldest street from the Golden Fleece pub, yet another of York's famously haunted locations.

property. I then ended up doing an impromptu reading for Simon's friend, Barry. It's odd really, as I was trying to tune in to the building but a dog then came through. It was a brown Boxer dog that had a bad paw. It would always hobble around on three legs and was very ill indeed. When I mentioned this, Barry nearly fell over; you see, the brown Boxer dog was Barry's. It died not so long ago with a number of afflictions. One was that it had problems breathing, and the other was that he had lost the use of one of his legs! I never knew this, and Barry was astounded. Also, when we were down here earlier on, we all heard footsteps and thumps coming from the rooms above … well nobody was up there at the time and the buildings either side of this property are empty, so what could it have been? I also get the feelings of aches and pains, and sores around the mouth.

At this point, I caught a glimpse of something moving from the corner of my eye. It was on the stairwell landing and it moved very quickly. I said nothing. Just as I was about to turn and look towards the stairs to see what it was Ralph said, 'there you go again, there is more movement over there.' He pointed directly to the door where I had just caught the movement. It turns out we both saw something and I was quite surprised to say the least. Ralph tied up his thoughts by saying:

> I am dying to get down to the bottom end, to Number 22. Just walking down The Shambles, the atmosphere, and the sensations you've got here are just second to none. We are going to get some activity tonight, I can feel it. We had a little bit so far, so I am looking forward to what the rest of the night may bring.

My preliminary interviews were complete and I knew all I needed to know insofar as we knew where we should place our motion sensors and trigger objects.

During the course of these tests, while making our way down the stairs to the lower section of the building, the most unusual thing occurred. Drew's EMF meter began to show a high reading

Inside the gift shop at number 22 The Shambles. Objects are reported to be thrown around by 'unseen hands' and it is under this very floor where the cellars and tunnels are located.

The haunted stairwell in shop 44.

in an area where it shouldn't have. It was nowhere near the ceiling, nor was it near any walls, so hidden wires could be ruled out. As we progressed down the stairs (about five steps) the high reading persisted. We went back to the original site of the reading, five steps up, but now it had gone altogether! It appeared that the high EMF reading had come down the stairs with us! Then, when we thought it couldn't get any stranger, it happened again. Down a few stairs we went and where we had just had the high reading, nothing! And it was now in the spot where Drew was taking the new readings.

It seems that there was an anomaly within the natural electromagnetic field. An anomaly that seemed to be following us down the stairs. It baffled us all as to what could be causing this. I am not saying that this odd reading was detecting a ghost or spirit. We don't know that for sure. But there was very strange readings within the electromagnetic field where there shouldn't have been. It also just happened to be in the very area where the ghost of a woman has been seen; an interesting occurrence to say the least. We finished the baseline readings on the ground floor and, apart from the aforementioned oddity, all went well. We were now ready to begin our overnight surveillance.

Drew Bartley, Fiona Vipond and Simon Cox staked out the cellars in number 22 first, while the rest of the group focused on number 44. I stayed downstairs with Mark Winter and investigation guest Barry Mason, while Ralph Keeton and Paul Dixon investigated the top floor.

I began the vigil by taking some new temperature and EMF readings and it was pretty much the same as earlier on. I called out to the atmosphere to see if we could gain any responses from any of the spirits or ghosts that are thought to reside there, but to no avail. Mark Winter set up his video camera at the foot of the stairwell looking up. If anything or anyone should make an appearance on the stairs, hopefully Mark would catch it. One thing during this vigil did occur, however, which is worth noting. At around midnight, when I was walking through the door to return back into the main café area, I felt a succession of short, sharp tugs upon my lower trouser leg. It was a definite 'pull', as though someone actually grabbed my clothing.

Ralph and Paul had a little success in their vigil on the top floor. A few taps and bumps were heard throughout the vigil and one or two strange lights were filmed on video camera. Ralph had a little more to say in regards to his psychic impressions. He came downstairs and told us that he thought there was an old 'walkway' or alleyway that once led from the front of the shop in The Shambles to the rear of the building. He suggested that the alley may have been where the store cupboard was in the café area. In regards to the café section (or side) of the building, Ralph claims this may have been built later than the original building. He felt that where the café is now, was an area where people would gather or collaborate, only then it would have been outside.

This may link with the experience of Chantelle and her sister, who, if you recall, saw a man venture into this area and seemed to disappear where Ralph thinks the alley once was. Perhaps it was the shade of a man strolling around in his day, who decided to venture up an alleyway that, of course, isn't there anymore … it's an interesting thought.

Drew and Fiona had an interesting time in their vigil too, with some very odd K2 EMF readings in the cellar and tunnels. I grabbed Fiona during our first break and this is what she told me:

In the second cellar, the larger of the two, something touched me on the hip, full on. There was no one next to me at the time, so I know it wasn't any of the group. About ten minutes into the vigil, my camera started to play up, just like they were doing when we were all in here earlier on. So that was quite interesting. At around 11.50 p.m. Drew's EMF machine went off of it's own accord, so perhaps something, or some sort of energy, manifested itself there at that time? We swept that area again soon after and we got a reading of zero. Just before the end of the vigil I began to feel really unwell for some reason … perhaps I was disorientated down there, I don't know. I would have thought if I was, I would have felt sick earlier on, as opposed to near the end of the vigil. Our K2 EMF went berserk too. We got some rather interesting results after calling out down there. It was spiking quite a lot and giving a high reading. Every time it was asked a question it went off, but every time we stayed quiet, it stayed quiet – it was really odd. One final thing … just as we were leaving the cellar at the end of the vigil, Simon heard a horrible guttural breath. Definitely worth re-investigation.

So, not a bad start. After the break at 1.30 a.m., Ralph, Paul, and guest Barry paid the cellars a visit in number 22, while Mark and I investigated the top floor. Drew, Fiona and Simon staked out the café area. Disappointingly, not a thing was documented or experienced during the course of our vigil, but that's what happens when you are ghost hunting – more often that not you don't hear or see a thing. Mark and I did hear one loud tap during our vigil, but put it down to natural causes. A floorboard contracting or the wooden beams in the ceiling settling down; nothing paranormal. EVP experiments were carried out with no results worth noting.

When Ralph and Paul returned from the cellars I asked Ralph about what (if anything) had occurred. Ralph told me:

In shop 22 we had a little bit of activity. The first cellar was rather quiet, so after a while we moved into the second cellar. When we got in there we spent a little bit of time discussing things. After we began the investigation, we took out the K2 EMF and swept the area. Now three lights came on, two green and one orange. Now wherever we swept with the K2 the energy remained. Like with you guys on the stairs earlier on, when we took a reading where we had just took the reading earlier on, it was now gone! It was as though the electromagnetic field anomaly was following us around, it was so strange. I established the fact that there was a young girl in there and for some reason she was

Drew Bartley taking some very peculiar readings on the stairwell at shop 44. The EMF anomaly seemed to follow us down the stairs as we went, disappearing from the area we had just surveyed.

Mark Winter carrying out electronic voice phenomena experiments (EVP) in the top floor of shop 44.

frightened. Then I became aware of the guy in there, Dan, and his presence was rather dominant. Every time we had contact with these spirits the lights on the K2 were on … but when I said, 'I think we are going now' (to Paul and Barry) the lights on the K2 went off and stayed off. It was as though the spirits there faded away as they knew we were off … weird.

At 2.30 a.m. I ventured outside alone to smoke a cigarette and by now thick, white snowflakes had begun to fall. The Shambles was completely deserted, and, as I gazed down the ancient cobbled lane, I could see the Christmas lights and festive decorations flashing. The two old crooked buildings that almost touch in the centre of The Shambles made the scene and for a moment I was transported back to Dickensian England. I half expected to see a Victorian gentleman with top hat and tails scurry round the corner blowing into his hands to keep them warm, or perhaps hear an old horse and cart making its way up the old cobbled lane. Brief moments like that are for me what it's all about, it was a moment I will never forget. It is also one of the reasons why I love ghost hunting so much.

After leaving the underground tunnels in shop 22 earlier on in the night (after taking a pre-investigation peek in there), paranormal investigator Mark decided to leave his EVP machine recording. By the time he left the shop, thirty minutes or so had already been recorded (while we were all in there) and by the time the first of the investigators arrived, another sixty minutes had passed, making the total time of the recording ninety minutes. The last sixty minutes of this recording is the most interesting as we know for a fact the premises was completely empty!

It starts twenty-seven minutes and thirteen seconds in with the voice of someone saying 'Help'. Now, we were all in the cellar at that time and no one – as far as any of us can remember – said the word 'help'. Granted, it could have been one of the investigators so we can't be 100 per cent sure. What we can be sure of is that the rest of the 'anomalous' sounds are totally unexplained – as the last sixty minutes of the recording no one was in shop 22 at all. Thirty-five minutes and fourteen seconds into the recording you can hear footfalls, and lots of them! Some close to the machine, indicating they are inside the cellar area, and some far away, suggesting that perhaps someone was walking overhead along the road above. It's more than likely the case that some of these footsteps do indeed have a natural cause, but it's just as likely (after hearing them) that some of them are truly anomalous. They are just too close to the recording device. A minute or so later (at thirty-six minutes and fifty-seven seconds), you can hear another eight footsteps, again very close to the microphone. At fifty-three minutes and nine seconds, three more footfalls are heard. Nine minutes later (at one hour two minutes and twelve seconds in), you can hear a voice saying 'Hello'. One hour and fourteen minutes and eleven seconds in another gruff voice is heard saying either 'Mary' or 'Nearly'. I personally think the voice sounds like it is saying 'Mary', but this is open to interpretation. Two minutes later (at one hour sixteen minutes and eleven seconds), a distinct and harrowing growl is heard – chillingly similar to the howl that is so often reported in shop 44. Finally, at one hour twenty-two minutes and thirty-five seconds, you can hear the last voice of this recording, and it simply says, 'Dead'.

They were harrowing recordings to say the least and I make no judgement or claims regarding them. They are what they are ... eerie recordings made in an alleged haunted property. Hearing them sends chills down the spine and, for me, it seems that they add to the evidence that is forever building of the existence of the supernatural.

Time was getting on now, and it was decided that we should pack up our gear and head off home. The fact that we were all beginning to tire was another reason for calling it a night. Tiredness can have a detrimental effect upon investigators and any anecdotal evidence of any kind, such as feelings of sickness or being touched, and seeing or hearing things, can be seriously flawed.

The Shambles. (Darren Olley)

To spend a night on York's Shambles searching for its ghosts at Christmas time is something that no one to this day has ever done, not in a scientific sense anyway. It was an honour and a privilege to be part of a unit that can now lay claim to being the first people in history to investigate not only two properties on York's oldest street, but the tunnels and cellars underneath it.

THE CHRISTMAS SPIRIT

Christmas comes but once a year,
The Yuletide spirit permeates the air.
The birth of Christ we celebrate;
A spiritual time, to contemplate.

Christmas is a time for living,
A time for gifts and joyous giving.
A time for peace, goodwill and love,
A time for prayer, to the lord above.

The festive season has more than this:
Snow and ice – and family bliss.
Sitting up late, till past midnight,
Telling ghost tales, by candle light.

Spectres abound, they roam the land
As Christmas Day becomes close to hand.
A fright or a warning, is their unearthly mission,
There walks through a wall, a gaunt apparition.

You tremble with fear, can't believe your eyes,
This wasn't expected, it was a surprise!
Have you just glimpsed the walking dead?
Or was it all, merely in your head?

You stop and think, you take a breath,
Does this alter your perception of death?
Seasonal greetings, to the guests you host
And Christmas wishes, to your resident Ghost.

Darren W. Ritson

BIBLIOGRAPHY

BOOKS

Hallowell, Michael. J., *Christmas Ghost Stories* (Amberley Publishing, 2008)

Hallowell, Michael J., *Invizikids, the Curious Enigma of Imaginary Childhood Friends* (Heart of Albion Press, 2007)

Haining, Peter, *Ghosts* (BCA, 1974)

Hallum, Jack, *Ghosts of the North* (David & Charles, 1976)

Hapgood, Sarah, *500 British Ghosts and Hauntings* (Foulsham, 1993)

Harries, John, *The Ghost Hunter's Road Book* (Letts, 1968)

Hippisley Coxe, Antony *Haunted Britain* (Pan, 1973)

Jones, Richard, *Haunted Inns of Britain and Ireland* (New Holland, 2004)

Kirkup, Rob, *Ghostly Northumbria* (The History Press, 2008)

Lyndon Dodds, Glen, *Historic Sites of Northumberland and Newcastle-upon-Tyne* (Albion Press, 2002)

MacKenzie, Andrew, *Hauntings and Apparitions* (Heinemann, 1982)

Maple, Eric, *Supernatural England* (Hale, 1977)

O'Donnell, Elliot, *Haunted Britain* (Rider, 1948)

Poole, Keith B, *Haunted Heritage* (Guild Publishing, 1988)

Puttick, Betty, *Supernatural England* (Countryside Books, 2002)

Price, Harry, *Poltergeist Over England* (Country Life Ltd, 1945)

Ritson, Darren W., *Haunted Newcastle* (The History Press, 2009)

Ritson, Darren W., *Ghost Hunter, True Life Encounters from the North East* (GHP, 2006)

Ritson, Darren W., *In Search of Ghosts, Real Hauntings from Around Britain* (Amberley, 2008)

Ritson, Darren W., *Supernatural North* (Amberley, 2009)

Stead, W.T., *Real Ghost Stories* (Grant Richards, 1891)

Underwood, Peter, *This Haunted Isle* (Harrap, 1984)

Underwood, Peter, *A Gazetteer of British Ghosts* (Souvenir Press, 1971)

Underwood, Peter, *The A-Z of British Ghosts* (Chancellor Press, 1992)

WEBSITES

http://nli.northampton.ac.uk/ass/psych-staff/sjs/blackdog

Rickard, J. (10 April 2001), Battle of Edgehill, 23 October 1642, http://www.historyofwar.org/articles/battles_edgehill.html

http://www.quotegarden.com/christmas.html

Index

Other titles published by The History Press

Ghost Hunting: A Survivor's Guide
JOHN FRASER

This book sets out to be a practical guide to ghost hunting. Examining cases from the distant past and the present day, John Fraser asks if it is possible to find the truth in this age-old quest. A detailed history of the three major paranormal societies is complimented by advice on which one to join, and when. If you have ever wondered how to organise your own ghost hunt, a list of essential equipment and a step-by-step guide to choosing your ideal spooky location is also included.

978 0 7524 5414 6

Ghost-Hunter's Casebook
BOWEN PEARSE

Andrew Green, who died in 2004, was for sixty years one of Britain's most active and best-known ghost-hunters. The most important cases from his lifetime of research are collected together in this volume – alongside new research and many reports that have never previously been published. This is an essential guide to the career of Britain's most famous ghost-hunter, and indeed to the paranormal history of 'our haunted kingdom'.

978 0 7524 4500 7

Tales from the Terrific Register: The Book of Ghosts
ED. CATE LUDLOW

As a schoolboy, Charles Dickens took a copy of the *Terrific Register* every week, and he later recalled how it 'frightened my very wits out of my head, for the small charge of a penny weekly.' This selection contains all the finest ghost stories from this 185-year-old publication. With countless reports of apparitions and premonitions of all kinds, extraordinary instances of second sight and visitations from spirits predicting fortunes, deaths and dreadful disasters, it will chill all but the sturdiest of hearts.

978 0 7524 5416 0

The Great British Christmas
MARIA HUBERT

This is a delightful history of how Christmas has been celebrated in Britain over the past 2,000 years. Amongst the wealth of stories and personal reminiscences this book also teaches us how the traditions we now hold so dear came into being, including Mrs Beeton's recipe for the original Christmas cake (made with a horn of mead), the birth of Christmas carolling, the first ever Christmas tree to be brought to England from Germany by Prince Albert and the origins of the Christmas cracker.

978 0 7524 5322 4

Visit our website and discover thousands of other History Press books.
www.thehistorypress.co.uk